IMAGES OF WAR

M36/M36B1 Tank Destroyer

IMAGES OF WAR

M36/M36B1 Tank Destroyer

RARE PHOTOGRAPHS FROM WARTIME ARCHIVES

DAVID DOYLE

Pen & Sword
MILITARY
AN IMPRINT OF PEN & SWORD BOOKS LTD.
YORKSHIRE – PHILADELPHIA

First published in Great Britain in 2019 by
Pen & Sword Military
An imprint of
Pen & Sword Books Ltd
Yorkshire – Philadelphia

ISBN 978 1 52674 892 8

A CIP catalogue record for this book is available from the British Library.

Typeset in 12/14.5 Gill Sans by
Aura Technology and Software Services, India

Printed and bound in China by Printworks Global Ltd

Pen & Sword Books Limited incorporates the imprints of Atlas, Archaeology, Aviation, Discovery, Family History, Fiction, History, Maritime, Military, Military Classics, Politics, Select, Transport, True Crime, Air World, Frontline Publishing, Leo Cooper, Remember When, Seaforth Publishing, The Praetorian Press, Wharncliffe Local History, Wharncliffe Transport, Wharncliffe True Crime and White Owl.

For a complete list of Pen & Sword titles please contact

PEN & SWORD BOOKS LIMITED
47 Church Street, Barnsley, South Yorkshire, S70 2AS, England
E-mail: enquiries@pen-and-sword.co.uk
Website: www.pen-and-sword.co.uk

Or
PEN AND SWORD BOOKS
1950 Lawrence Rd, Havertown, PA 19083, USA
E-mail: Uspen-and-sword@casematepublishers.com
Website: www.penandswordbooks.com

Contents

Acknowledgments

This book would not have been possible without the generous assistance and resources of many friends and institutions. Among them, Rob Ervin, Don Moriarty, David Fletcher, Joe DeMarco, Pierre-Olivier Buan, John Blackman, Chris Hughes, David Levy, Joe McClain, Reed Knight, Mike Koening, Scott Taylor, the late Jacques Littlefield and the former staff of the Patton Museum. Special thanks to my wife Denise.

INTRODUCTION

Going into the Second World War, the prevailing strategy of US command was that tanks were not to be used to engage enemy tanks in combat. Rather, tanks were to be the armored spearhead to breach enemy positions. Enemy tanks were to be dealt with by specialized weapons, aptly named tank destroyers. Early on these were 37mm towed anti-tank guns. These were soon found to be inadequate against enemy armor, and the quest for larger weapons began, as did the desire for a self-propelled anti-tank gun – or Gun Motor Carriage. After initial efforts, which involved adapting ¾-ton Dodge trucks to mount anti-tank weapons (the M6, née WC-55) or half-tracks (the M3 75mm Gun Motor Carriage) attention turned to utilizing a tank chassis as the basis for an anti-tank weapon.

Two failed attempts were made to mount the 3-inch gun in the modified hull of an M3 medium tank. By January of 1942 a prototype was in the works to mount the weapon in an open-topped turret on the chassis of the twin GM Diesel-powered M4A2 Sherman medium tank. After some months of development a design was finalized for a vehicle sharing the suspension, lower hull, and engine with the M4A2 but with an upper hull made up from thinner, but sloping, armored plate. It was hoped that the weight savings would produce increased automotive performance. Initially designated T35E1, when the design was standardized it was redesignated M10. In addition to the 6,700-plus Diesel-powered M10 tank destroyers, a further 1,700 M10A1 vehicles were built, these being driven by Ford GAA gasoline engines.

While the 3-inch weapon of the M10 was superior to that found on earlier US tank destroyers, it was still found to be inadequate against the ever-increasing weight of German armor. The British addressed this by rearming some of the 1,700 M10s that they received with the superb 17-pounder quick-firing anti-tank cannon. From May 1944 through April 1945, 1,017 of these vehicles were converted at various Royal Ordnance Factories. They were designated by the British as 17-pdr M10 SP Mark IC. After the war they were given the name Achilles.

The US, also seeking heavier armament, created a new turret, mounting a 90-mm gun. Beginning in April 1944 the new 90-mm armed tank destroyer, designated M36, entered production. These vehicles were built new, from 100 new hulls purpose-built for this, and by remanufacturing M10A1s, primarily from US-based training units. As the supply of these chassis was depleted, additional vehicles were created by converting Diesel-powered M10s, resulting in the M36B2. The M36B1 was built from the ground up as a tank destroyer, using a hull based on that of the M4A3 but featuring a standard M36 turret. Examination of rare surviving vehicles indicates that the M36B1 hulls were manufactured expressly for this purpose, and were not merely M4A3 hulls converted.

While US anti-tank doctrine changed, rendering all the tank destroyers obsolete after the Second World War, many of these vehicles were supplied to other nations, and in fact some survived as combat vehicles into the twenty-first century.

When wartime experience showed that the 3-inch gun of the M10 tank destroyer was ill suited to combating the increasingly heavy armor of German tanks, the US Army moved to adapt the M1 90mm anti-aircraft gun to a tank-destroyer chassis. A modified 90mm gun designated the T7 (later standardized as the M3) was installed in the first pilot M10 tank destroyer, and that combination is seen during tests at Aberdeen Proving Ground in November 1942. (Patton Museum)

CHAPTER 1

M36

As seen in a comparative photo of an M10, left, and a 90mm Gun Motor Carriage M36, USA number 40177413, both vehicles had similar hulls, but the turret of the M36 was a new design, larger than that of the M10 to accommodate the bulkier gun, and with a prominent bustle built into the rear of the turret. The heavy bustle served as storage space for eleven rounds of 90mm ammunition and also acted as a counterweight to offset the mass of the front-heavy gun. (Patton Museum)

Train-load M-10A1 3 in. Gun Motor Carriages being unloaded for re-build & conversion to M-36, 90MM Gun Motor Carriages

Above: Massey-Harris was one of several companies to do conversion work on M36s. The vehicles in the foreground here are at that plant at the beginning of the hull-assembly process. The first several chassis on the right have their transmission covers removed. In the background, a chassis is being hoisted. (NARA)

Opposite above: The pilot for the M36, the 90mm Gun Motor Carriage T71, was equipped with a ring mount for a .50-caliber machine gun above the left side of the turret. Arranged at intervals on the hull plates were bosses for fastening proposed supplementary armor plates. This vehicle had the type B207881 variation of the model D47527 bogie assemblies with open-spoke wheels, and the model D47366A drive sprockets. (Patton Museum)

Opposite below: To allot chassis for the new M36 tank-destroyer program, the final production lot of 300 M10A1 chassis was diverted for conversion to T71s. Soon the Army decided to divert already completed M10A1s to the M36 program. Seen here are completed M10A1 tank destroyers being delivered by flatcars for conversion to 90mm gun motor carriages. (NARA)

Massey-Harris workers are installing fans in an M36 engine compartment. In the foreground is the turret ring. The fixture on the bulkhead below the ring with the rubber hose above it is the transmission oil cooler, with a guard made of metal slats to protect it. (NARA)

Mechanics are lowering a Ford GAA V-8 engine into the hull of an M36, while other GAAs to the right await installation in other chassis. These engines replaced the less powerful General Motors 6046 engines installed in the M10 tank destroyers. The GAA was an eight-cylinder model with a displacement of 1,100 cubic inches. (NARA)

A US Army Ordnance officer, Lieutenant Foster L. Boutillier, inspects a line of M36 tank destroyers that have been repaired or refurbished by Ordnance repair units in France. The scene was the base of the 25th Battalion, First Army Ordnance, near Hirson, France, on 18 September 1944. These hulls lack the bosses for supplemental armor, an indication that they were converted from M10A1 chassis built in July 1943 or later. (NARA)

Members of a US Army tank-destroyer unit pose on their M36s while training with the vehicles somewhere in France in October 1944. The two closest vehicles have thread-protector rings fitted on the 90mm gun muzzles, to protect the threading on the barrels for installing muzzle brakes. The farthest M36 lacks the ring: an indication that this was one of the first 600 M36s produced, as they lacked provisions for a muzzle brake. The nearest M36 has suffered damage to its fender. (NARA)

An M36 tank destroyer is poised on a street in Metz, France, on 11 November 1944, the day after the city was captured from the Germans. The vehicle was assigned to Company C of the 607th Tank Destroyer Battalion. Secured to the fronts of the rolls on the side of the turret is a metal bucket. (NARA)

Occasionally M36 tank destroyers suffered the indignity of being used as field artillery, as was the case of this vehicle of Company C, 702nd Tank Destroyer Battalion, Ninth Army, on 16 December 1944. The vehicle is parked under camouflage netting strung from poles, and extra netting is draped on the hull. The tank destroyer rests on an earthen ramp to increase the elevation of the 90mm gun. (NARA)

M36s of Company C, 702nd Tank Destroyer Battalion, are emplaced on earth ramps preparatory to shelling enemy targets across the Roer river on 16 December 1944. The firing positions were well prepared, with pits for storing 90mm ammunition to the rears of the tank destroyers. (NARA)

Moving through thick fog are M36s of a tank destroyer battalion cooperating with the 82nd Airborne Division near Werbomont, Belgium, during the Battle of the Bulge, on 20 December 1944. The closest vehicle and the one following it have their 90mm guns cradled in bow-mounted travel locks instead of the stock rear-mounted locks. This modification was intended to allow the crew to get their gun into action towards the front as quickly as possible. (NARA)

Above: An M36 tank destroyer that has strayed from a road and become stuck is being recovered. The turret is traversed to the left, and the large bustle at the rear of the turret is hanging over the right side of the hull. The sprocket is the D47366 'economy' type, solid, without cutouts around the inner rim. (NARA)

Opposite above: In the winter of 1944-5 in northwestern Europe, it was common for crews of US armored units to camouflage their vehicles with whitewash; it disguised the vehicles in snowy terrain and was relatively easy to remove at the end of winter. Here Corporal Theodore Herbert applies a coat of whitewash to an M36 tank destroyer in Luxembourg on 3 January 1945. Most of the whitewash job is quite neat, but at this point Corporal Herbert is splashing the whitewash from a bucket onto a bogie assembly. (NARA)

Opposite below: A white snowsuit-clad member of the US Army Engineers stands next to a whitewashed M36 tank destroyer of the 602nd Tank Destroyer Battalion near Dudelange, Luxembourg, on 3 January 1945. A canvas muzzle cover is in place on the 90mm gun. (NARA)

An M36 tank destroyer attached to the 702nd Tank Destroyer Battalion has slipped off an icy road and rolled over an embankment near Fisennes, Belgium, on 5 January 1945. One crewman was killed and another was severely injured in the accident. The vehicle was being towed to an ordnance repair depot at the time. (NARA)

The same M36 is seen from another angle, facing the front of the vehicle, before a tank retriever moves in to recover it. The steel T54E1 tracks with their prominent treads had not kept the vehicle from sliding on ice and careening over the embankment. On the bow of the hull is a bundle of logs, for use in unditching, with the added bonus of protection from anti-tank rounds. (NARA)

Above: In a final view of the aftermath of the crash of an M36 near Fisennes, medics carry away the remains of the dead crewman while other GIs prepare to get the vehicle on its way to the repair depot. In the far left of the photo is an M26 6x6 armored tractor seen from the rear. (NARA)

Opposite above: In the third photo of a series, a tank-recovery crew has fixed steel cables to the M36 tank destroyer near Fisennes on 5 January 1945, in an effort to stabilize and then right the vehicle. (NARA)

Opposite below: The recovery crew has righted the M36, which, aside from the disarray of the logs on the bow, looks little the worse for wear. However, even slight damage to many systems of the M36, from the 90mm gun barrel and mount to the suspension and the mechanical components, could render the vehicle unserviceable. To the side of the vehicle, medics cover the body of the crewman killed in the crash. (NARA)

Above: Just south of Langlir, Belgium, on 13 January 1945, an M36 passes an abandoned Pz.Kpfw. IV tank with its right track missing. The M36's 90mm gun was a match for the armor of the German heavy tanks, and the gun was more than a match for the lighter-armored Pz.Kpfw. IV. (Patton Museum)

Opposite above: A US Army M36 in the foreground works with several tanks, including two Sherman medium tanks and several M5A1 light tanks in the distance, somewhere in northwestern Europe in early 1945. With its 90mm gun, the M36 had a far meaner punch than any US tanks except the T26E3 Pershings that saw combat in small numbers in the final weeks of the war in Europe. (NARA)

Opposite below: An M36 tank destroyer of the 2nd Armored Division, foreground, cooperates with a column of Sherman medium tanks on a snowy, hilly stretch of road outside Dochamps, Belgium, on 10 January 1945. Snow-covered camouflage netting is arranged around the hull and the turret, which would have tended to confound enemy recognition of its type at a distance. (Patton Museum)

In the snowy, sometimes wet weather of the winter of 1944-5 in northeastern Europe, it didn't take long before whitewash camouflage began to wash off, as seen on this M36 tank destroyer. Streaking of the whitewash is visible on the hull, and the original Olive Drab paint is showing through on the turret bustle and the 90mm gun barrel. Note the curved cutout in the hull above the idler wheel, no doubt a field modification to ease the build-up of mud on the track. (Patton Museum)

Infantrymen, a Sherman tank, and three M36s, part of the 104th Infantry Division, occupy a street in Düren, Germany, on 24 February 1945. The M36s probably were assigned to the 692nd Tank Destroyer Battalion, which at that time was operating with the 104th Division. This battalion had just received its M36s that month. (NARA)

Forces of the 5th Armored Division, Ninth Army, stream through Hardt, Germany, on 2 March 1945. Following the Jeep are two M36 tank destroyers. The front M36 has what appears to be a thick plank and a pole, or possibly a tow bar, on the bow. (NARA)

The crew members of an M36 tank destroyer of C Company, 771st Tank Destroyer Battalion, maintain a watch while supporting the 102nd Infantry Division in Krefeld, Germany, on 3 March 1945. A good view is available of the .50-caliber machine gun and mount; the barrel is secured in the travel lock. Also visible is the prominent thread-protector ring on the muzzle end of the 90mm gun; this was one of two models of thread-protector rings observed on the guns of M36s in the Second World War, being a design with thicker diameter. (NARA)

Above: An M36 tank destroyer with a large white star on the glacis is parked between a Jeep and a Dodge weapons carrier in the village of Gorpdorf, Germany, on 5 March 1945. In the foreground is a dead German soldier. (NARA)

Opposite: Members of the 11th Infantry Regiment, 5th Infantry Division, Third Army, stream past M36 tank destroyers that are temporarily delayed by road blocks ahead, outside Reisweiler, Germany, on 8 March 1945. Each of the first two M36s has, as a modification, a plate welded to the upper part of the mantlet to shade the gun-sight aperture. (NARA)

Above: Members of the crew of an M36 tank destroyer wait expectantly for an ambulance to arrive to evacuate an infantryman on a stretcher on the ground, who has just lost a leg to a land mine. A .50-caliber machine gun and a .30-caliber machine gun are atop the turret. Holders for five-gallon liquid containers, evidently fabricated from welded steel rods, are on the glacis plate. A modification seen here is the travel lock on the bow, for facilitating bringing the gun into action to the front as quickly as possible. (NARA)

Opposite above: Among the vehicles of the 76th Division, Third US Army, that are advancing through Speicher, Germany, on 7 March 1945, is an M36 in the foreground. In addition to the normal equipment stowed on the exterior of the vehicle, there are a number of crates and boxes on the rear deck, and a box, partially covered by a tarpaulin, is mounted on the rear of the turret bustle. (NARA)

Opposite below: An M36 tank destroyer occupies a position between some battle-damaged buildings in the town of Rimling, France, during the advance east in March 1945. The .50-caliber machine gun on the turret has a dust cover over it. Unit markings appear to be present on the fronts of the fenders but are unreadable because of glare. (NARA)

Above: The crew of M36 40191415 nicknamed 'Pork Chop' take a break during the US advance, in the outskirts of Oberwesel, Germany, on 18 March 1945. According to the original caption of the photo, this vehicle was assigned to the 2nd Cavalry Regiment, Third US Army. Fitted on the 90mm gun muzzle is a variant of the thread-protector ring used on guns threaded for muzzle brakes. This type of ring was hat shaped, with a thin-walled main component flaring to a wider diameter at the rear. Adjoining that ring to the rear and separated from it by a washer was a nut with a key for proper alignment of the muzzle brake when installed. The nut and the flared rear portion of the protector ring were of the same diameter. (NARA)

Opposite above: A column of vehicles of the 3rd Infantry Division, Seventh US Army, advances along the Baddurkheim–Ludwigshaven highway in Germany on 23 March 1945. At the center is an M36 tank destroyer with a front-mounted travel lock for the 90mm gun. A .30-caliber machine gun and ammunition box are present on the left front of the top of the turret: a type of mount that became increasingly common, as the .50-caliber machine gun on the turret bustle proved ill-suited for use against ground targets, being difficult to maneuver and leaving the gunner fully exposed much of the time. Holders for five-gallon liquid containers are on the glacis. (NARA)

Opposite below: In late March 1945, an M36 of the 45th Infantry Division, Seventh US Army, is emplaced alongside a stone house in Nieder-Wurzbach. Red and white striped aiming stakes, for use in indirect-fire missions, are jammed behind the grouser rack on the side of the hull. The bogie wheels and idlers on this vehicle are the solid type. (NARA)

Mutual destruction may have been the backstory of this Jagdpanther and M36 tank destroyer lying side by side in a field along a railroad track, knocked out of action near Kaimig, Germany, on 17 March 1945. The Jagdpanther has two large punctures in its armor to the rear of the superstructure, while the M36 has a large rupture in its sponson, and one of the hatch covers has landed upright on the ground next to the forward bogie assembly. (NARA)

Because of the vulnerability of the crew in the open turret of the M36 to enemy fire and splinters, in August 1944 the Army Ground Forces ordered that work commence on an armored cover kit. One of those kits is shown here being tested on an M36 turret at Camp Hood, Texas, in late January 1945. Twelve supports held the top of the cover nine inches above the top of the turret to give the crew headroom and a means of looking outside. The cover plates were 3/8-inch armor, and the outer edges of the cover were angled downward. (Patton Museum)

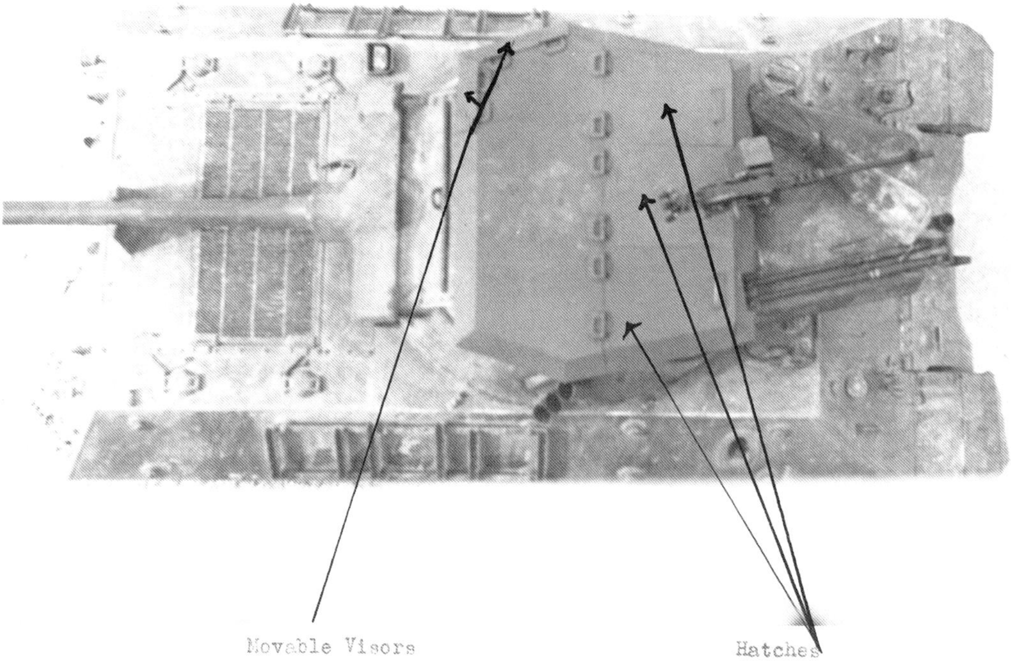
Movable Visors
Hatches

Above: As seen in an Aberdeen Proving Ground photo on 5 May 1945, part of the deep-water fording kit was this air-intake adapter that was installed over the grille over the engine compartment. The air-intake trunk would then be mounted on this adapter. (Patton Museum)

Opposite above: The armored cover is viewed from above. On the rear half of the cover were three hatch doors, each of which had two hinges to the front. At the front right corner of the cover were two hinged visors, one at the front and one at the side; opening them gave the gunner a larger field of vision. (Patton Museum)

Opposite below: Development of a deep-water fording kit for the M36 was accomplished by April 1945, and an M36 with the kit installed is seen here from the rear during tests at Aberdeen Proving Ground on 7 August 1945. The main elements were two extension trunks: the front one was an air intake, and the rear one carried away exhaust gasses. (Patton Museum)

Above: An M36 tank destroyer is backing onto the ramp of an LCM (landing craft, mechanized) before being ferried across the Rhine. The turret is fitted with an armored cover, atypical for the M36, with a vision slot on the side of it; the cover may have been an adaptation of the cover developed for the M10 tank destroyer. (US Army Engineer School History Office)

Opposite above: There was an adapter for the exhaust trunk of the deep-water fording kit for the M36, as seen from under the adapter facing forward in a 5 May 1945 photo. On the bottom of the adapter was a door with a grab handle, held in place by clips. To each side of the adapter is an idler mounting bracket. The purpose of the frames extending from the rear of the hull on each side of the adapter is not clear. (Patton Museum)

Opposite below: In April 1945 the US Army mounted a major effort to move men, vehicles, and equipment across the Rhine during the final push into Germany's heartland. Seen here is an M36 tank destroyer of the Third Army being ferried across the river on an assault raft. (US Army Engineer School History Office)

340

Above: Both of the M36 tank destroyers in this photo of the ferrying operation on the Rhine have sandbag 'armor' on their glacis plates. The vehicle to the left has in addition a tattered sheet of fabric stretched over the sandbags. Attached to the tarp is a piece of paper marked 'A/CT4', apparently routing instructions. A clear view is available of the shield plates of the turret cover; the two side plates each have a vision slot, while the frontal plate has three vision slots. (US Army Engineer School History Office)

Opposite above: On 6 April 1945 an M36 is being prepared for loading onto a landing craft for transport across the Rhine. This vehicle has the same type of turret cover as the M36 in the preceding photo. Note the pointed design of the front of the turret cover and the vision slots in the side plates of the turret cover. (US Army Engineer School History Office)

Opposite below: The LCM to the right has reached the shore and dropped its ramp, and the M36 to the left is ready to back down the shore to the landing craft. Whereas the turret cover on the M36 in the preceding photo had vision slots in the side plate and the next one to the front of that plate, the cover in the photo lacks the vision slot in the latter plate. (US Army Engineer School History Office)

Three M36s of the 628th Tank Destroyer Battalion, assigned to the 5th Armored Division, are parked on a street in Rheydt, a few miles west of the Rhine river in Germany. All three vehicles have nonstandard turret covers with vision slots as well as a .30-caliber machine gun mounted towards the left front of the turret roof, in addition to the standard .50-caliber machine gun towards the rear of the turret. (Patton Museum)

An M36 tank destroyer is emplaced as a static pillbox, situated in a dugout entrenchment. This position would give the vehicle good protection against all but direct hits or airbursts, but would negate two of the M36's chief assets: speed and mobility. The 90mm gun barrel has the thin-diameter variant of the thread-protector ring, with a nut to its immediate rear. (US Army Engineer School History Office)

Above: Infantrymen accompany an M36 tank destroyer during an advance in the European theater towards the end of the war. The turret bustle is piled particularly high with equipment and bedrolls, and local camouflage in the form of evergreen tree branches have been placed on the hull. (Patton Museum)

Opposite above: An M36 sits in the wreckage of a railroad station. By appearances, the vehicle has been knocked out. The right fender is crumpled, debris is lying on the vehicle, there are signs of wreckage in and on the turret, and the left suspension appears to be damaged. (Patton Museum)

Opposite below: During the drive east near the end of the war, an M36 tank destroyer passes a row of damaged houses. An abundance of gear is stowed on the turret and on the rear deck, some of it covered with a tarpaulin. On the left side of the turret top, a helmeted head is visible behind a .30-caliber machine gun. These machine guns, mounted in the fronts of the turrets, were a modification born of the need to deal with enemy threats to the front, in which direction it often was difficult or impossible to bring the more powerful .50-caliber machine gun into play. (NARA)

Above: Two side-by-side M36 tank destroyers of the 601st Tank Destroyer Battalion and Sherman tanks of the 756th Tank Battalion are doing duty as battle taxis, loaded with foot soldiers of the 3rd Infantry Division preparatory to an attack on Wetzhausen, Germany, on 9 April 1945. At least the closer M36 has 'duckbill' end connectors on the outsides of the tracks for extra flotation, and the lower extension of the sponson has been cut away to give clearance to the duckbills. This photo serves as a good comparative illustration of the thicker-diameter thread-protector ring on the muzzle of the 90mm gun on the left M36, and the thinner-diameter thread protector ring on the vehicle to the right. Both versions had a nut to the rear of the thread-protector ring, but the nut is more noticeable with the thinner-diameter ring. (NARA)

Opposite above: A man in an overcoat, possibly a displaced person, flashes the 'V for victory' sign at the crew of a passing M36 of the 9th Armored Division, First US Army, at Naumberg, Germany, on 13 April 1945. A plank has been secured between the fenders to hold stowed gear on the glacis. This vehicle's turret had a front-mounted .50-caliber machine gun. (NARA)

Opposite below: Two M36 tank destroyers of the 87th Division cross a pontoon bridge over the Saale river in Germany on 14 April 1945. The closer vehicle has a .50-caliber machine gun on a pintle mount in the front left corner of the turret. On the glacis is a section of spare track, a solid-disk bogie wheel, and other gear. (NARA)

Above: An M36 tank destroyer supports infantry of the Ninth US Army who are covering an intersection in Tangermünde on 12 April 1945. A stowage rack is on the rear of the hull with a tarp thrown over its contents. An armored cover with vision slots is present on top of the turret. (Patton Museum)

Opposite above: Infantrymen of the Ninth US Army engage enemy forces in Tangermünde, on the Elbe river in Germany, on 12 April 1945, while an M36 tank destroyer covers the area in the opposite direction. The M36 has a turret cover with vision slots, and a .30-caliber machine gun is installed on the turret in addition to the .50-caliber. (NARA)

Opposite below: The crew of an M36 takes a break from the action during the final drive into Germany on 12 April 1945, to shoot craps on a blanket to the rear of their vehicle. The name of one of the crewmen, Corporal Harold, is stenciled on one of the duffel bags strapped to the rear of the hull. A captured German jerrycan is strapped to the side of the hull. (NARA)

1914
1918
USA
40191683

Above: The ultimate development of the tank destroyer was the 90mm armed M36; basically a conversion made to existing M10A1s which were powered by the Ford GAA Gasoline V-8. The design incorporated a completely new turret with power traverse and a large bustle used for ammunition stowage that finally resolved the imbalance problem of the M10. Towards the end of M36 production, conversions were also carried out on the Diesel-powered M10 hulls resulting in the M36B2. (Pierre-Olivier Buan)

Opposite above: GIs of the 3rd Infantry Division hitching a ride on an M36 stare at a mural commemorating Germany's role in the First World War, in Berchtesgaden, Bavaria, the home of Hitler's Eagle's Nest retreat, on 4 May 1945. This M36, US Army registration number 40191683, had a .50-caliber machine gun in an unusual position, on the right front of the turret. (NARA)

Opposite below: After the Second World War, the M36 continued to serve, seeing combat in the Korean War and being exported to some United States allies. This example, USA number 40191661, is shown in use by the 53rd Republic of Korea Tank Company. (Patton Museum)

This beautifully restored M36 is an extremely complete example with many accessories items that are often quite difficult to obtain. It was modernized post-war with the M3A1 90mm gun.

The right front fender is an assembly of numerous sheet metal parts. The fenders are hinged to allow them to be folded back. This was often done during shipping or transport to avoid damaging the fender.

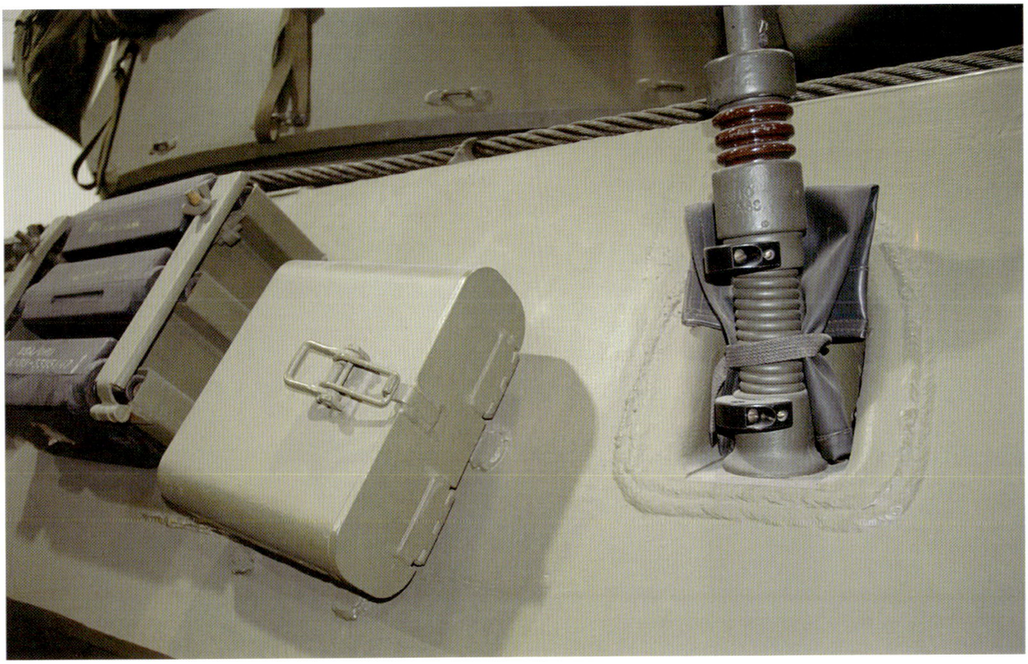

The antenna mount is installed into the recessed mounting bracket in the right front of the upper hull armor plate. The storage bag for the antenna base is attached to the aerial with a length of web strap.

The MP-48 base is made up of a mounting base plate, a spring, a porcelain insulator and the attachment point at the top for the aerial mast. The mast was assembled from 3 ft. lengths that screwed together.

The first aid box on the side of this M36 is a common fitting on many late war US produced AFVs. It was not included on all M36 production. The box holds a container for six field dressings.

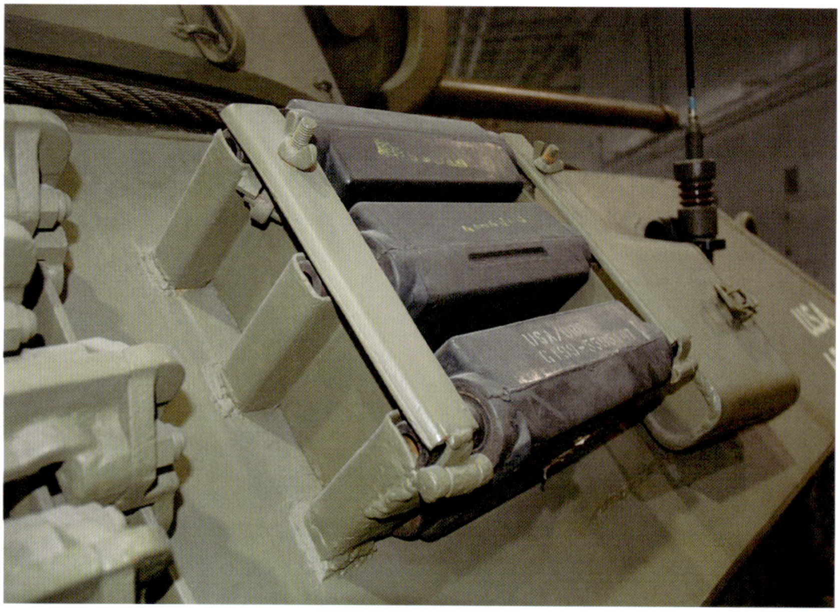

Another late production fitting is the rack for spare track blocks. These are the same brackets seen on late production M4 medium tanks. The new track blocks exhibit the flash from the mold for the rubber portion.

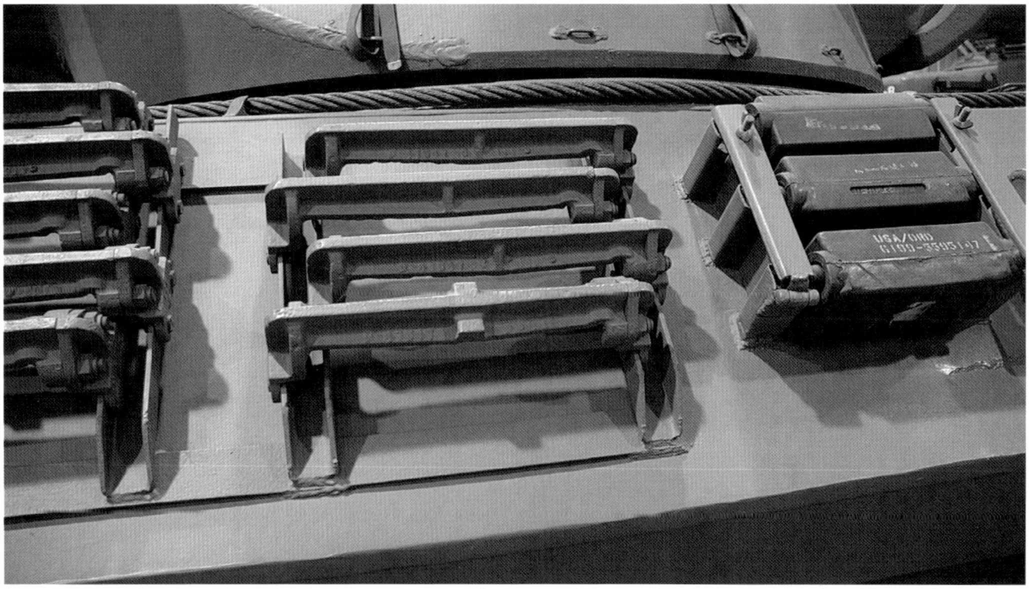

The M36 was equipped with the same track grouser stowage racks as the earlier M10. The rack on this vehicle no longer has the holes in the lower framework for mounting on the eliminated appliqué armor bosses.

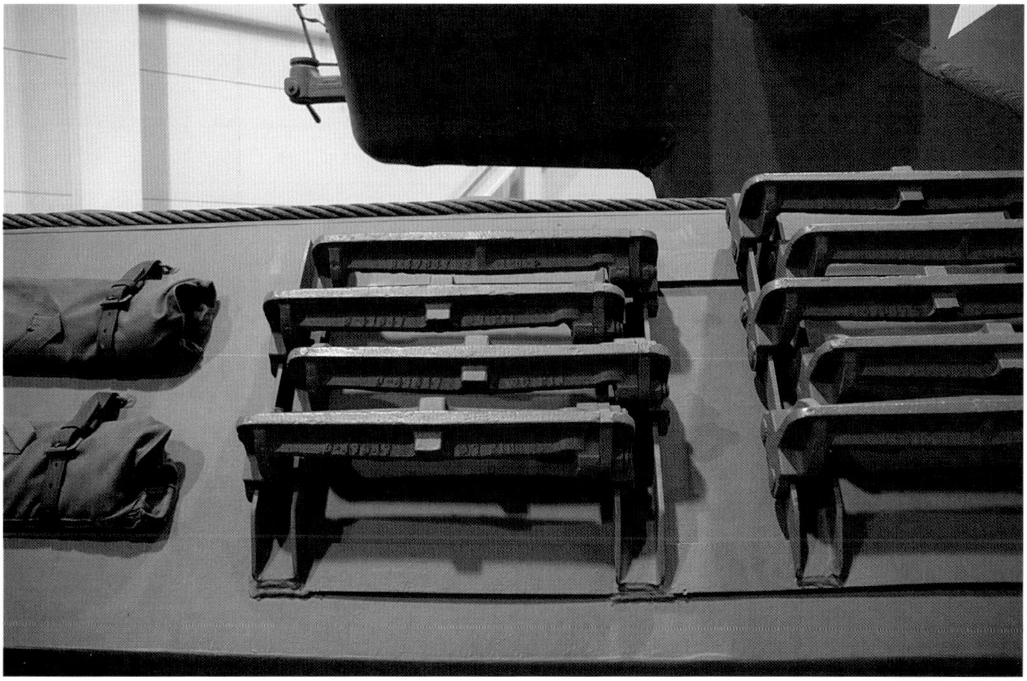

The grouser racks on this vehicle are full. The casting number details can be seen just below the cleat, with the part number to the left and manufacturer's numbers to the right side of the casting.

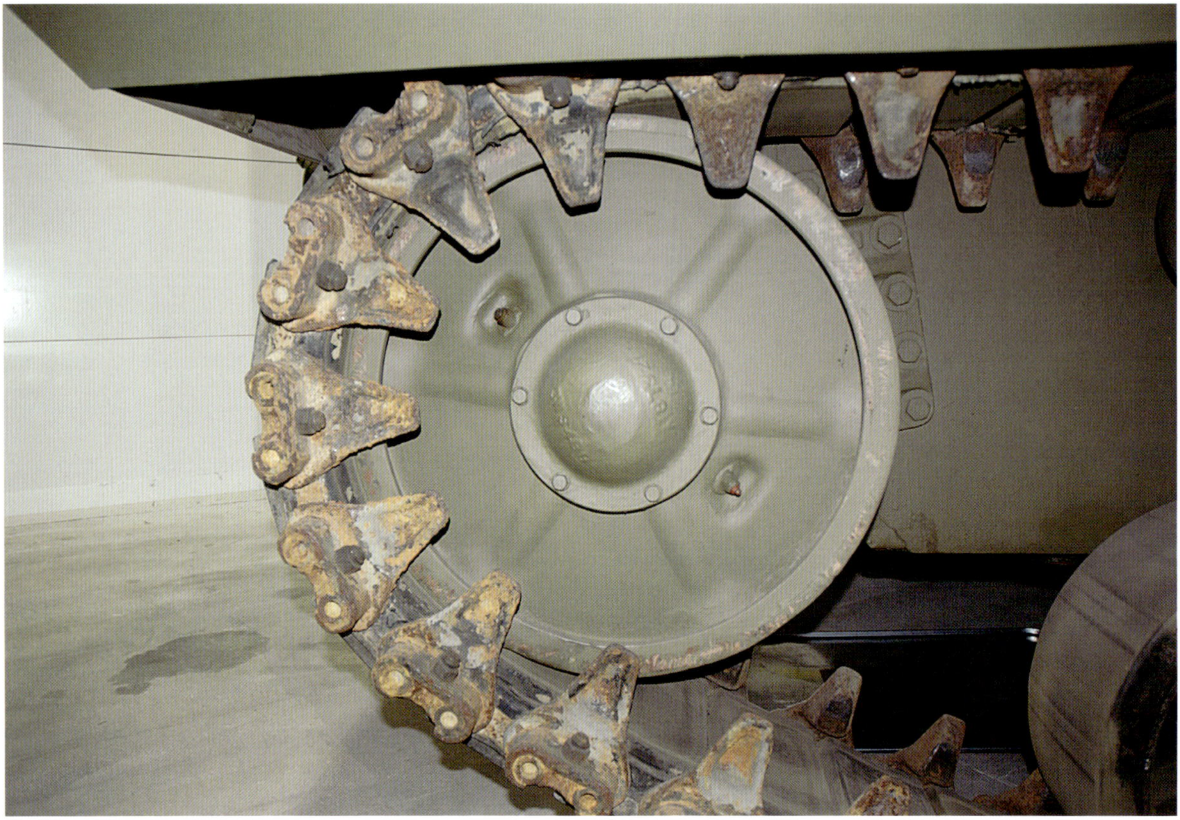

Above: The stamped idler wheel is a common sight on vehicles based on the M4 medium tank chassis. It has a cast tire portion with faces of the wheel made from steel stampings. Lubrication fittings are supplied for the hub.

Opposite above: The M36 shared the suspension bogies of the M4, this being a late style unit with the upswept bracket for the steel return roller. The right side wheel has had its openings filled with steel plate welded in place.

Opposite below: The track return roller is a steel casting which rides on a bearing against a center axle. The roller carried the weight of the track over the bogie units. The track end connectors have worn the paint from the roller.

Above: Drive sprocket plates were made for the M4 series in several styles; early castings, flame cut from steel plates, and later forged steel. This helped meet demand and the later styles were stronger than cast types.

Opposite above: Initially the M36 retained the 'U' shaped crutch style of travel lock from the M10. Later conversions received the longer A-frame type of gun travel lock that was similar to the designs used on the Sherman.

Opposite below: The installation of the gun travel lock on the rear plate required some repositioning of the pioneer tools compared to earlier models. The vehicle has a full complement of pioneer tools all painted Olive Drab.

2Δ
702TD
C 1

2Δ
702TD
C 1

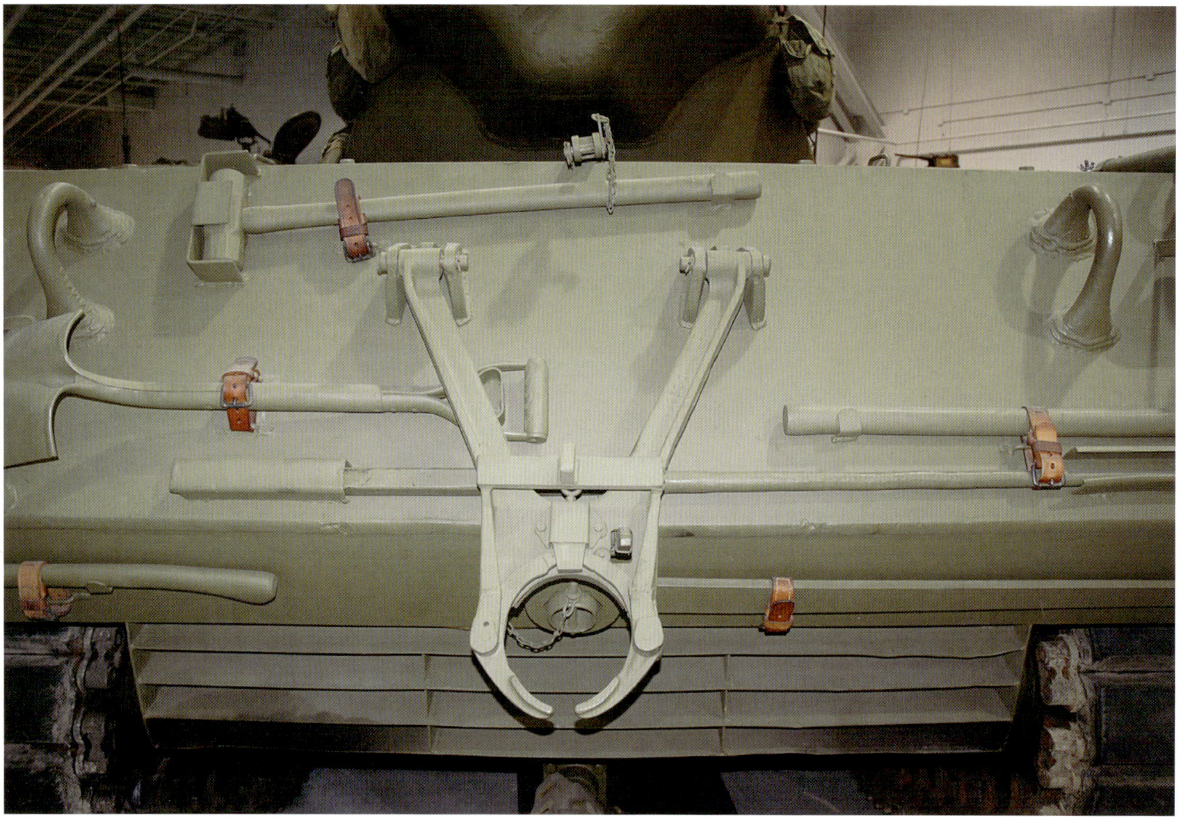

Above: The travel lock folds down to stow against the upper hull rear plate and a clip holds the lock in place against the hull. An additional retaining clip is at the center rear of the engine deck above the sledge.

Opposite above: The locking mechanism is a spring-loaded device that releases the jaws when the ring is pulled. The chain in the center of the jaws attaches the retaining pin for the track tensioning spanner seen behind the travel lock.

Opposite below: Below the left side tail light is the mounting bracket for the head of the shovel. The shovel head is a stamped and rolled piece of sheet steel and is a common design for use on US built vehicles up to the present day.

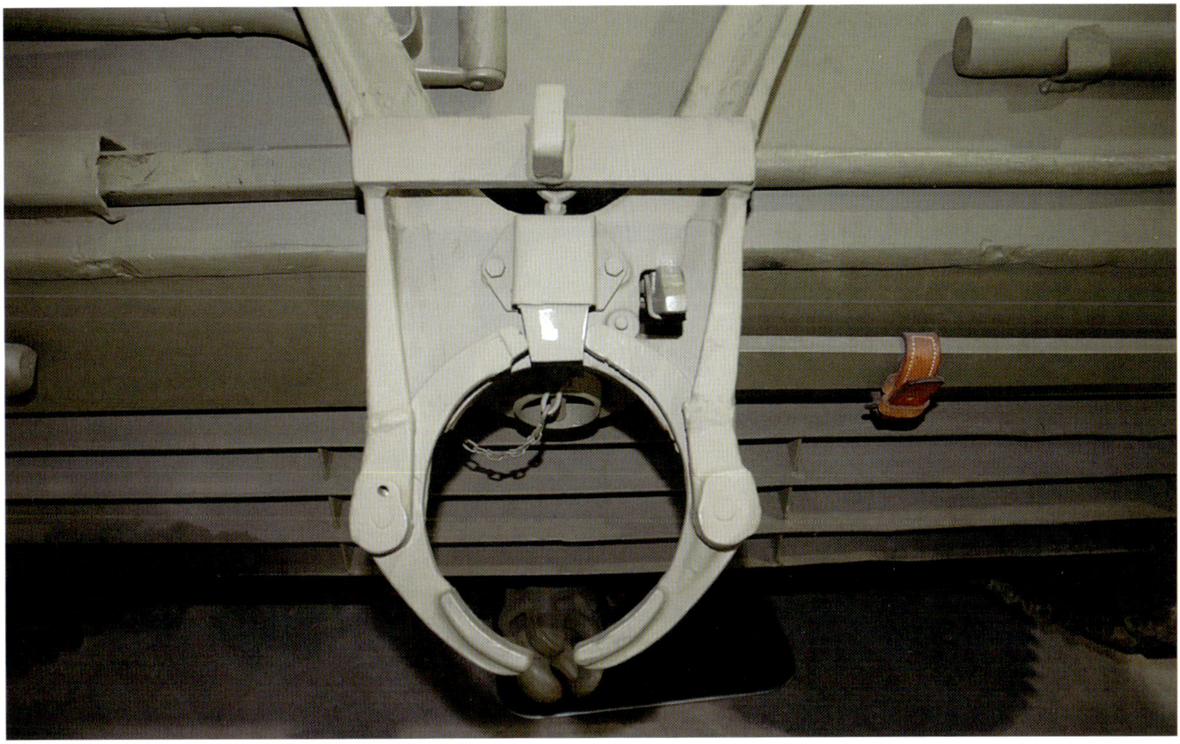

2Δ
702TD

Above: On the right side rear plate are stowed the mattock head, mattock handle, and track pry bar. The pry bar and mattock handle share a single footman loop to secure them. Below is the end of the tensioning wrench.

Opposite above: The GAA Ford gasoline engine was equipped with a sheet metal exhaust deflector redirecting exhaust and cooling air to the rear. This deflector is hinged to swing up for access to the engine door between the exhausts.

Opposite below: The exhaust deflector is a sheet metal structure that is the width of the lower hull. It has three internal vanes, the two exhausts plugging into openings in the bottom vane. It is very similar to the standard M4A3 part.

Above: Centered in the rear lower hull plate between the exhausts is a hinged access door for the engine compartment. Below the door on the plate is mounted a spring loaded towing pintle.

Opposite above: As is common on M4 based vehicles the later production vehicles are equipped with twin towing lugs on each side of the lower hull rear plate. Each vehicle carries a cable to attach to these lugs, normally with a clevis.

Opposite below: Carrying Canadian markings this M36 has been modified to accept the late style of armored exhaust deflector. Built up from sections of rolled plate these deflectors covered the weak areas of exhaust openings and the engine door. (John Blackman)

77

Above: The hull floor plate of the M36 has a single large access plate which when unbolted exposes the bottom of the large Ford V-8 gasoline engine. The Diesel-powered M10 and M36B2 has twin plates in this location.

Opposite above: The M36 was fitted with grab rails on the upper portions of the turret sides. They are often seen with the crew's gear stowed there strapped to them. This vehicle is fully stowed with the .50 Browning machine gun in its canvas cover on the turret bustle, and red and white ranging stacks on the right turret side. It lacks the right side hull grouser storage rack. (John Blackman)

Opposite below: The M36 was often used in roles for which it was not intended due to its potent 90mm gun. The thin frontal armor and lack of overhead protection for the turret made the vehicle vulnerable. The owner of this restored example has placed sandbags on the glacis that were often used in the later stages of the war in Europe to augment the thin frontal armor against German anti-tank weapons. (Pierre-Olivier Buan)

USA
40177412

Above: Many M36s converted from M10A1s were returned to the factories for rebuild; hence both early and late style differential covers are seen fitted. The late style has two tow-lugs per side.

Opposite: This dusty M36 has had the front fenders modified in a very common manner. The use of extended end connectors on the tracks made them so wide that they fowled the fenders; cutting them back to this shape solved the problem. (John Blackman)

Above: Clamps are provided at the front of the vehicle on the differential cover, and on the right rear of the upper hull for securing the vehicle's tow cable. The cable is the standard 20-foot length provided with medium tanks.

Opposite above: Initial production examples of the late sharp-nosed E8543 differential/final drive covers had crew steps incorporated into the castings outboard of the tow lugs. Later units have a welded step.

Opposite below: The left side tow-lug mounts a quick connect tow clevis. Common on late Second World War and post-war vehicles, the cable is slipped over the end of the clevis and rotated ninety degrees, locking the cable in place.

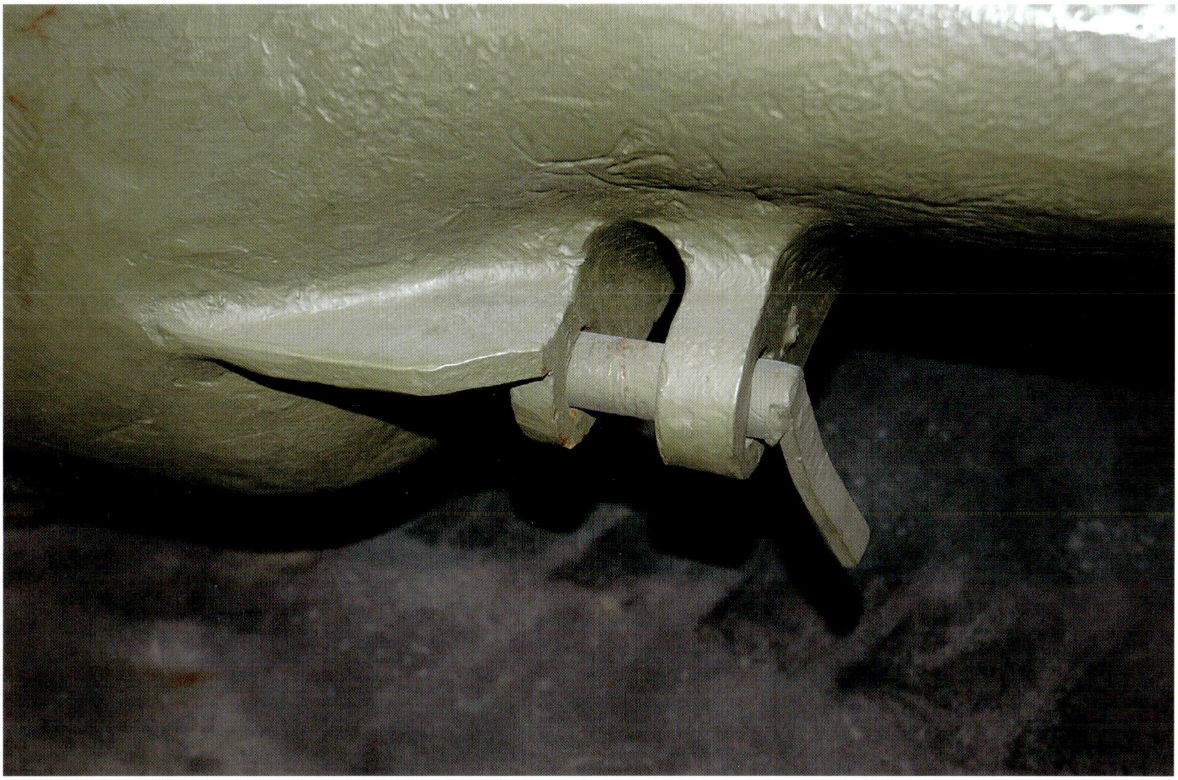

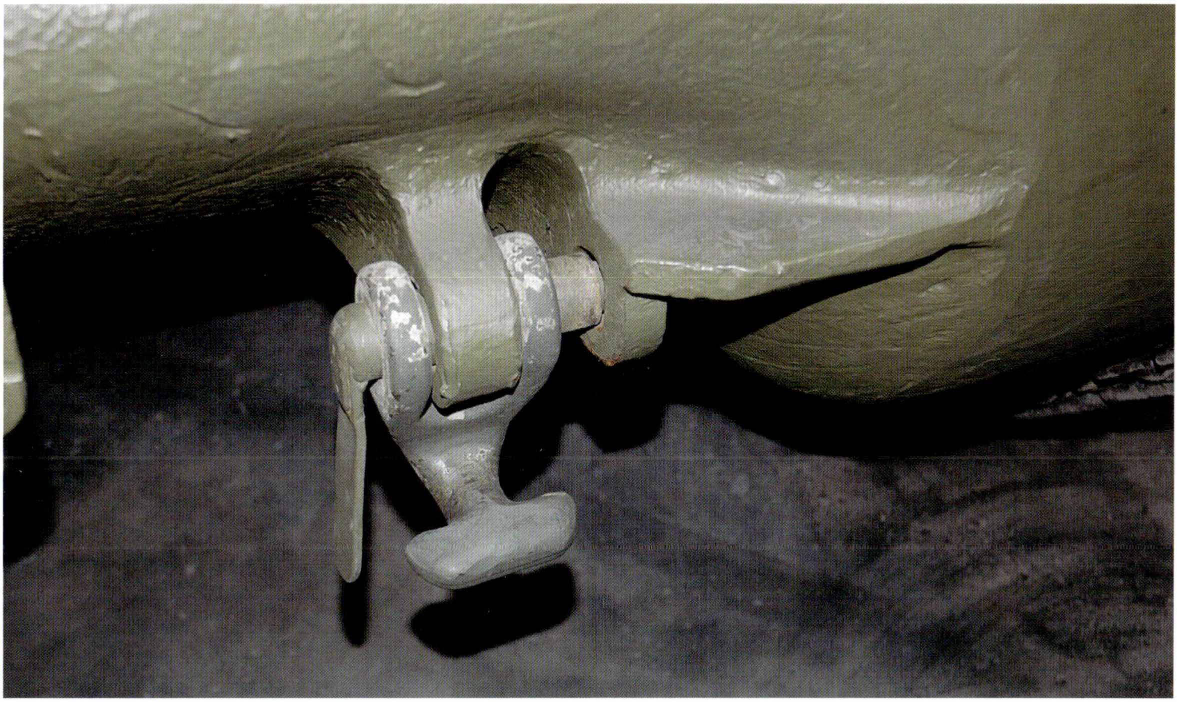

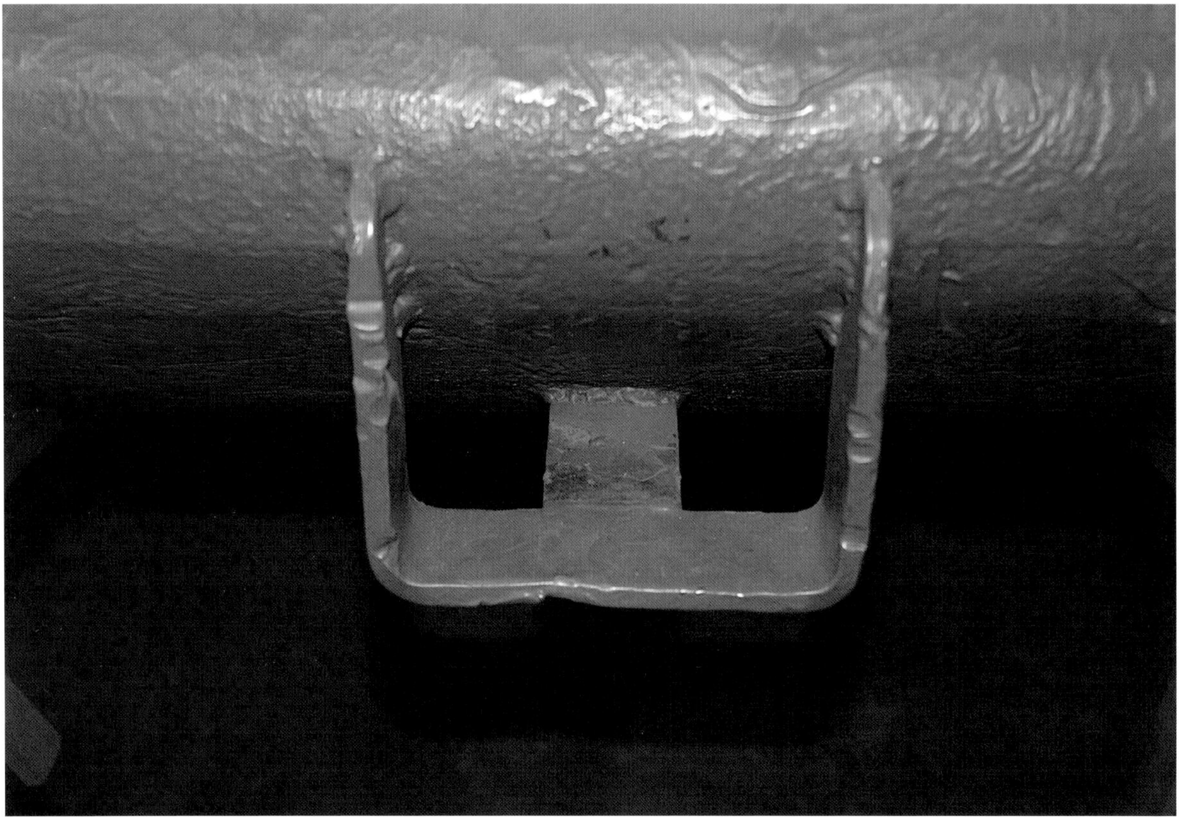

Above: Another fitting seen on tank destroyers which was not used on the M4 Sherman is a crew step in the center of the differential cover. The step is made from two pieces of flat bar stock welded to the cast cover.

Opposite above: The bolts that hold the drive sprocket plates to the central cast hub protrude slightly through the hub's flange. The worn paint on the rear sprocket shows the area where the track's end connectors make contact.

Opposite below: The prototype turret for the M36 incorporated a ring mount for the anti-aircraft machine gun similar to that on the M18 Hellcat. This was eliminated in production and a standard pintle mount was added to the roof of the turret bustle. This not only simplified production of the turret but made it possible to use the weapon while standing on the rear deck outside the turret, as seen here. (John Blackman)

USA
40177445-S

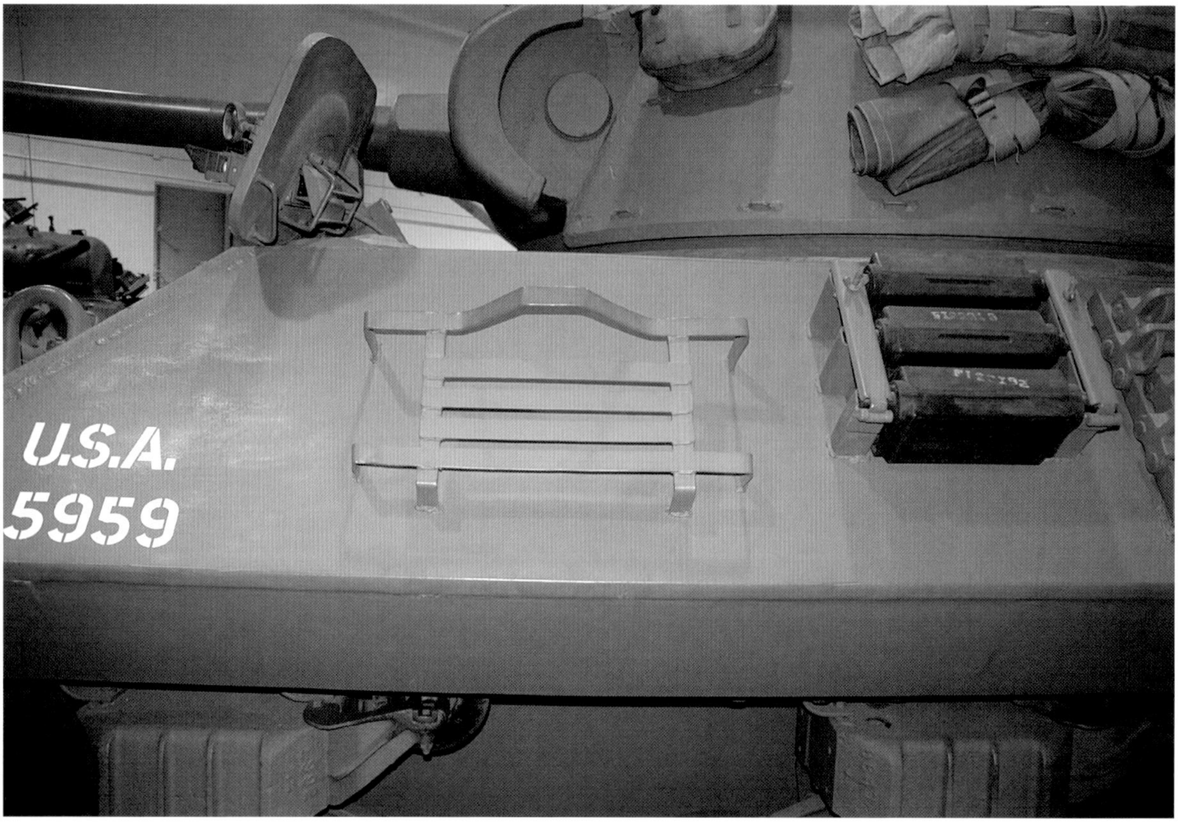

Above: A bracket for storing the foul weather driver's hood is mounted on the left side hull armor plate. The driver's hood was like a small convertible car top, with a windshield, defroster grid, and windshield wiper.

Opposite above: An additional spare track bracket and grouser stowage rack are welded to the left side armor plate. The grouser rack on this side has the holes in the lower brace that was used for mounting them on earlier hulls.

Opposite below: The engine deck doors are flanked by armored caps for the fuel fillers, each marked with an identification plate for 'gasoline'. The red handles in the box-like structure are the firing handles for the fire extinguishers.

D11

Above: Each armored fuel filler cap is a hinged steel casting with a pivot pin on one side and a removable pin on the opposite end. The removable pin is secured with a short section of chain to prevent its loss.

Opposite above: The fire extinguisher system of the vehicle was broken down to protect two areas: the engine compartment and the fighting compartment. Each had a fixed 10lb carbon dioxide bottle with nozzles around the compartment.

Opposite below: The hinged gun travel lock was held in place when erected by this strut that incorporated a turnbuckle. This prevented the travel lock from inadvertently falling down when the vehicle struck uneven surfaces.

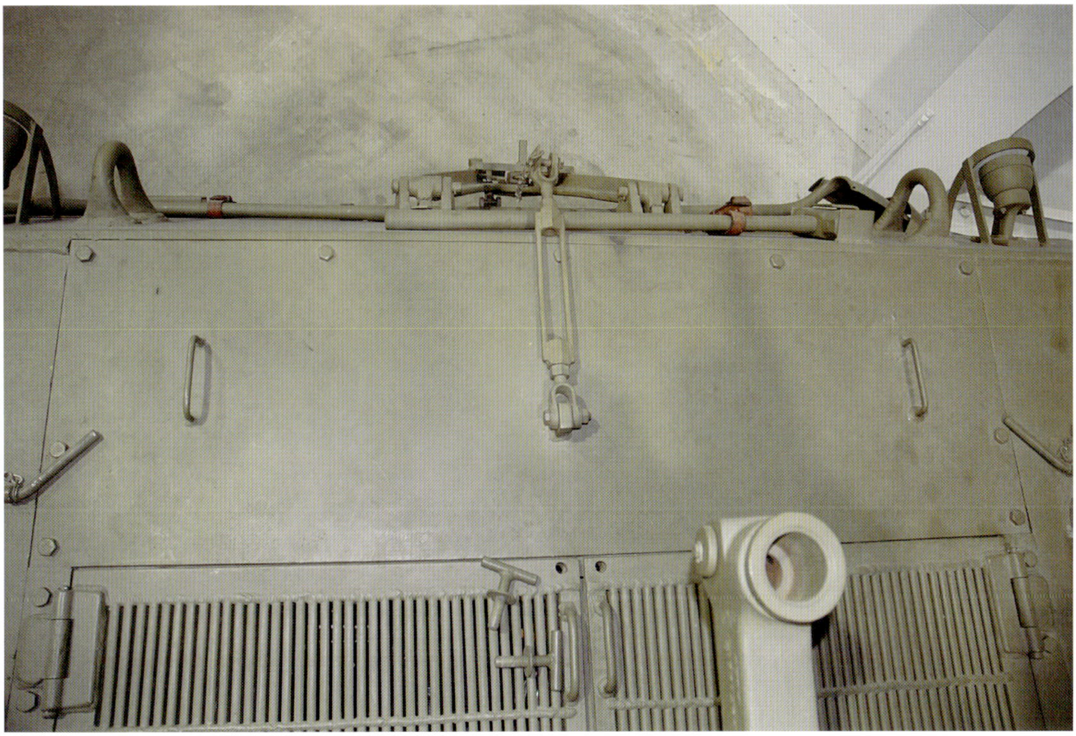

Above: The right side engine deck mounts the rear clamp for the tow cable. The fillers for the right side fuel tank flank the engine deck grill doors. The fuel tank capacity totaled 192 gallons providing an approximate range of 150 miles. The engine deck doors are constructed of pieces of steel rod welded to a framework of steel plate.

Opposite above: The engine deck doors are held closed by bolts at the center by the lifting handles. On early examples these bolts required a wrench for removal; this type can be removed by hand with the 'T' handle.

Opposite below: The large turret bustle served as a counterweight to the heavy gun as well as for ammunition storage. To properly balance the turret the bustle is nearly four inches thick in places. Note the large attaching weld beads.

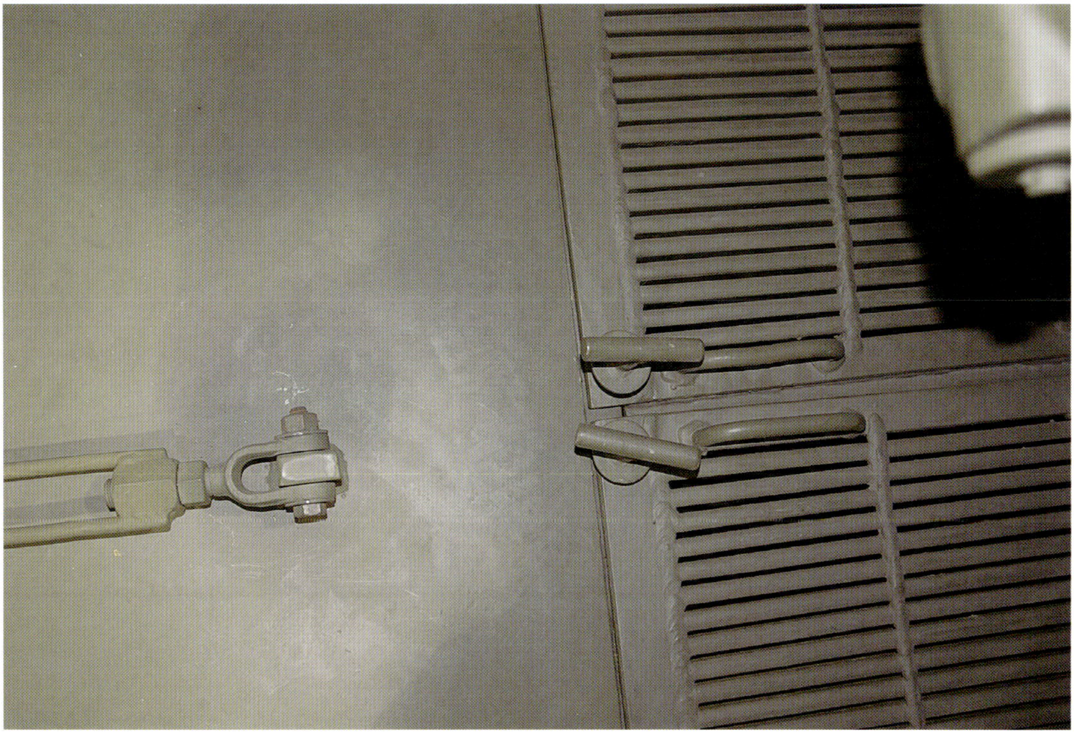

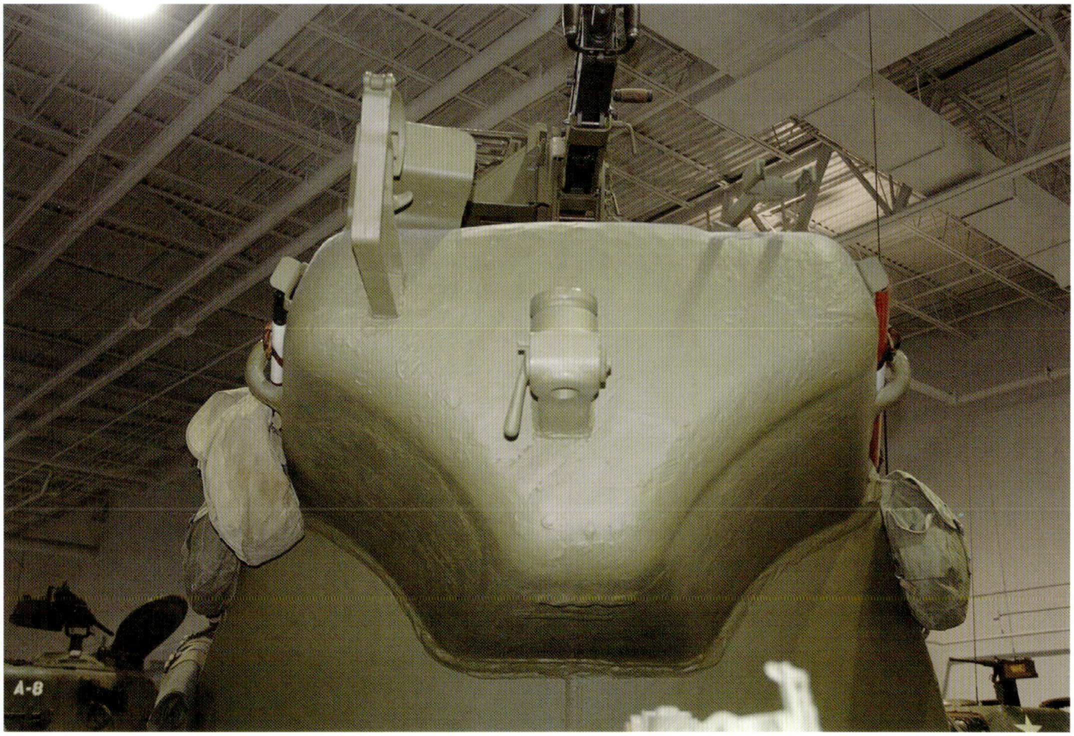

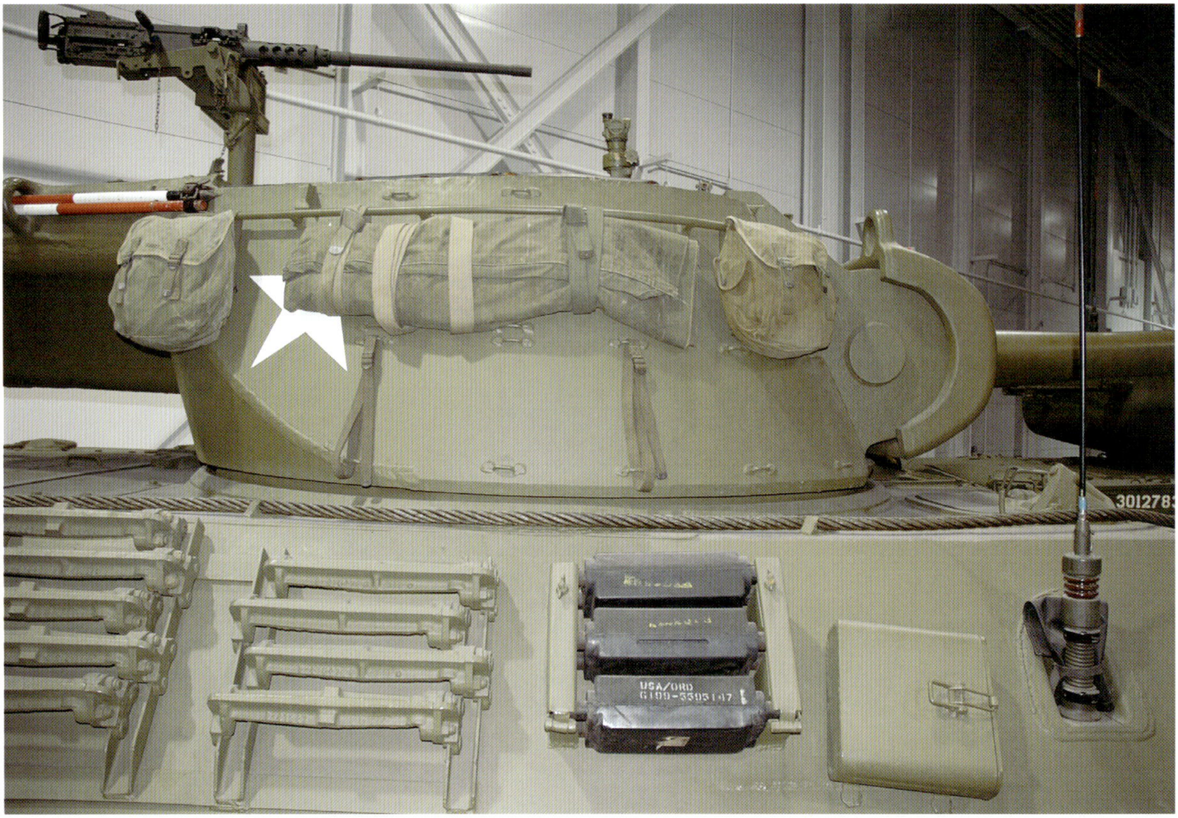

Above: The turret side walls are made of pieces of formed rolled armor plate welded together. Each exterior wall was fitted with a grab rail and a number of footman loops used for stowing the crew's personal gear.

Opposite above: The left side turret exterior is used here with more stowage attached, including musette bags, ground sheets, and ranging poles. The armor thickness of the turret walls was 1¼ inches, half an inch thicker than the M10.

Opposite below: The forward portion of the turret is made up of a large casting that carries the trunions, or pivot point of the gun mount. The casting marks are visible at the upper edge near the turret roof.

D11

Above: The gun shield is an armored casting with a maximum thickness of three inches. The collar covering the recoil portion of the barrel is an integral part of the casting. The opening at the upper right of the mantlet is for the gunner's sight.

Opposite above: The left portion of the glacis armor mounts a lift ring, headlight, headlight guard, and siren. Details of the hinged fender are seen above; the M6 periscope for the driver's hatch is at the lower center.

Opposite below: The contours of the assistant driver's hatch casting are evident when viewed from above. The hatch handle is angled across the front left corner. The swivel mount for the periscope is topped with a protective guard.

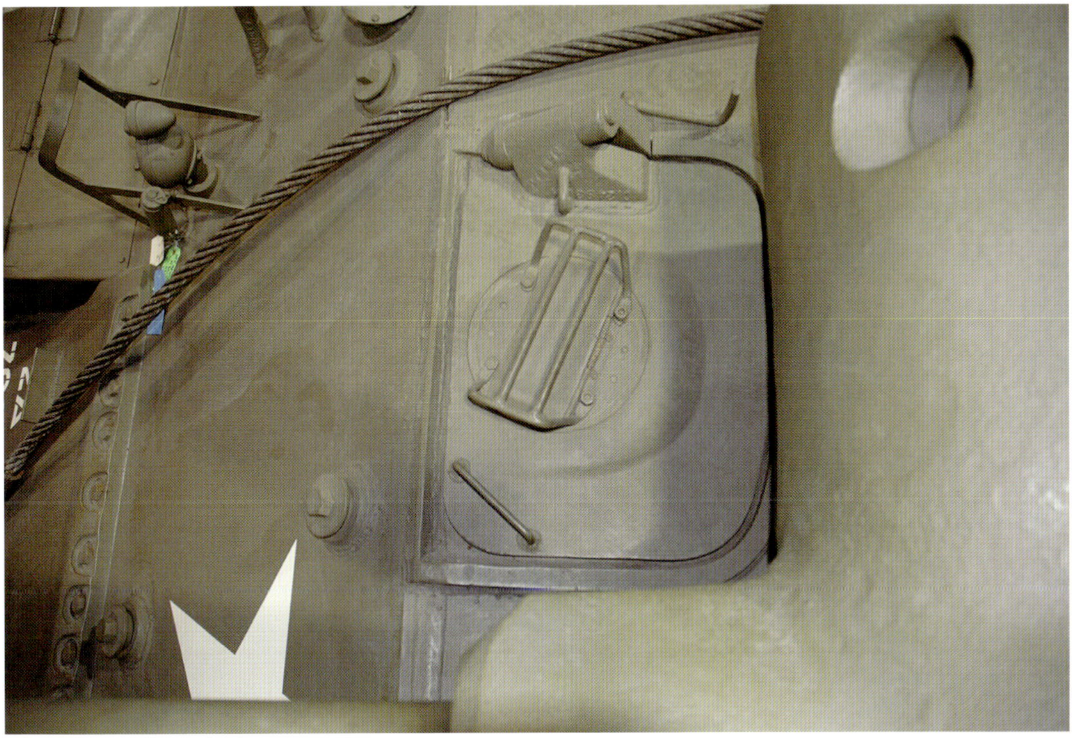

The partial turret roof is a cast part attached to the turret assembly with screws. This allows for removal of the gun for servicing. The four poles are supports for a tent-like canvas cover for the turret opening.

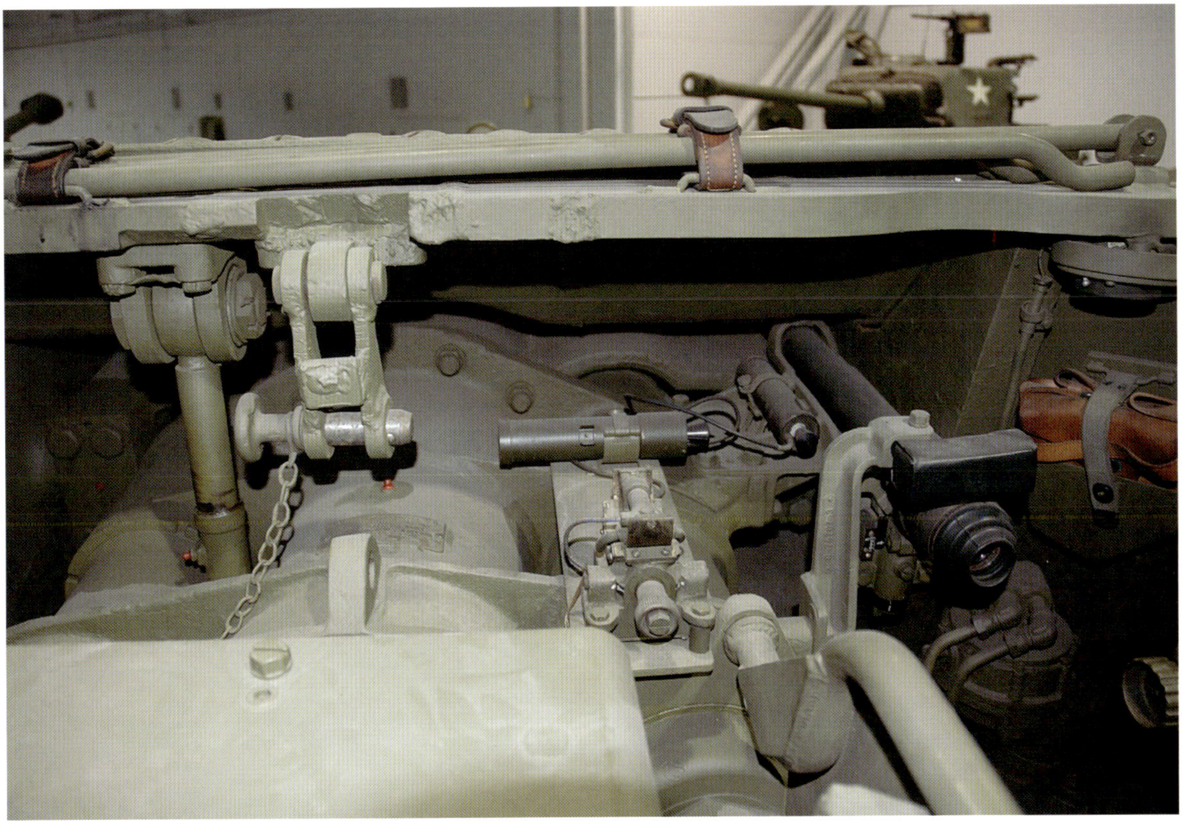

The front of the turret, the top of the 90mm gun, and the interior of the gun shield are viewed from above the breech. To the far left is a shaft that is part of the elevating mechanism, attached to the roof of the turret with trunnion bearings. To the right of it is the interior travel lock for the 90mm gun. Also to the right is the Telescope M76F on the Telescope Mount M64. The two tube-shaped objects to the left of the telescope, at right angles to each other, are instrument lights.

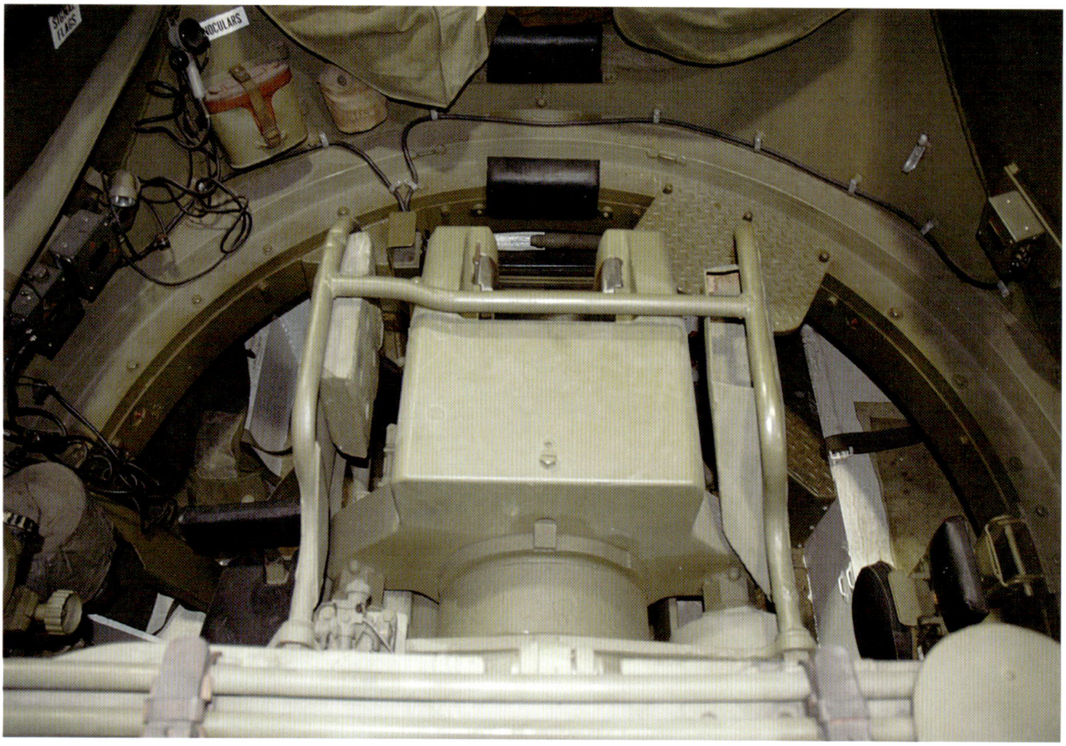

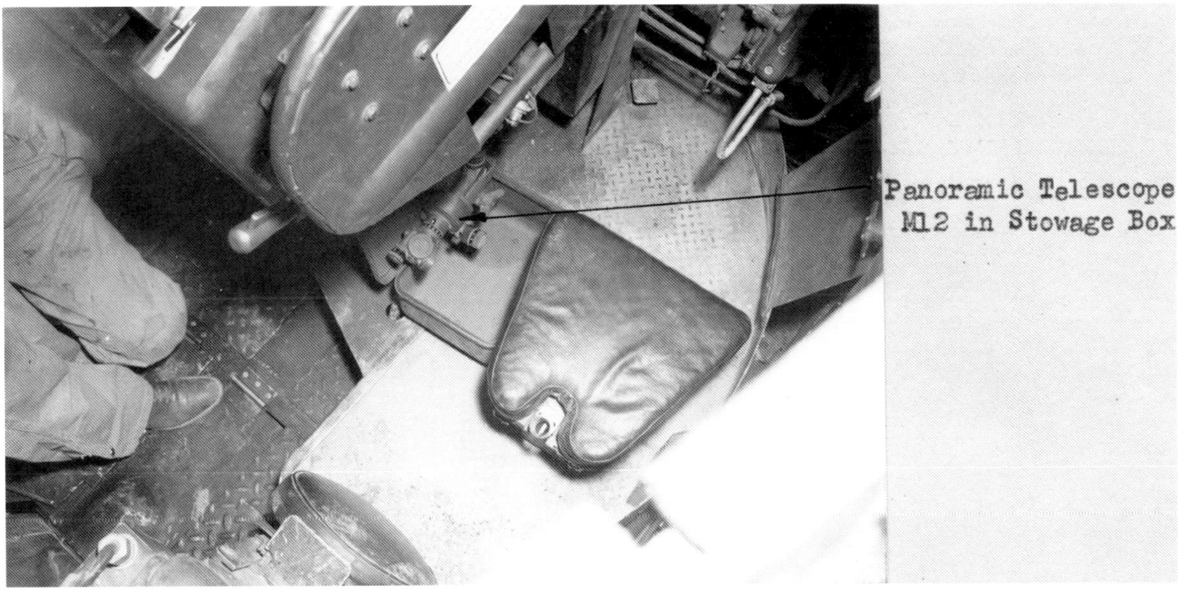

Above: In a photo looking down into the right side of the turret of an M36 tank destroyer, taken for the Tank Destroyer Board in May 1945, the gunner's seat is to the right, with the seat back removed. The 90mm gun breech is to the top, and on the floor below the breech is a Panoramic Telescope M12 in its stowage case. At the bottom is the folded seat for the commander.

Opposite above: The M36 is armed with the M3 90mm gun in the unstabilized M4 mount. It was the first US AFV to be equipped with this powerful weapon on the battlefield. Note the balance weights on the recoil guard.

Opposite below: To the right of the gun is mounted the M1 gunner's quadrant, used when the weapon was used in indirect fire roles. Many tank destroyers were used in fire support roles late in the Second World War as armored targets decreased.

Above: When firing at a target that cannot be seen – indirect fire – the panoramic sight is used to check alignment of the gun both horizontally and its elevation in relation to an aiming post placed in front of the vehicle.

Above: The M36 turret is provided with a hydraulic power traverse on the right side of the gun ahead of the gunner's position. This solved the traversing difficulty which had plagued the M10 throughout its production.

Opposite above: Looking to the rear of the turret the stowage for ready rounds in the bustle racks are protected by their canvas covers. Various points around the turret are padded for the protection of the crew.

Opposite below: Each member of the M36 crew is provided an interphone connection box to aid their communication. The headphones were mounted inside the crewmen's fiber and leather tanker's helmet

CULARS

SIGNAL
FLAGS
FLASHLIGHT
BINOCUL

Above: This vehicle is fully equipped with hand mics, flashlights, a signal flag case, canteen, and commander's binoculars case. The locations for many of the items are marked. Note the path of the interphone cabling.

Opposite above: In a photo taken for the Tank Destroyer Board at Camp Hood, Texas, on 18 February 1945, eleven rounds of 90mm ammunition are in the ready racks at the rear of the turret: six on the left side in three tiers, and five on the right side in two tiers. Each cluster of racks was provided with a canvas cover with a zippered closure flap at the front. Tank Destroyer Board tests in early 1945 demonstrated that these covers, particularly the flaps, were a nuisance and easily damaged, and the report of the tests recommended deleting the covers. On top of the left side of the turret bustle are holders for spare barrels for the .50-caliber machine gun. To the left is a holder for binoculars. (National Archives)

Opposite below: The large turret bustle casting was equipped with two racks for eleven ready rounds of ammunition storage. The zippered canvas covers kept the rounds protected from moisture. A wool blanket is stored between the racks.

U.S. ARMY SIGNAL CORPS
CAMP HOOD TEXAS

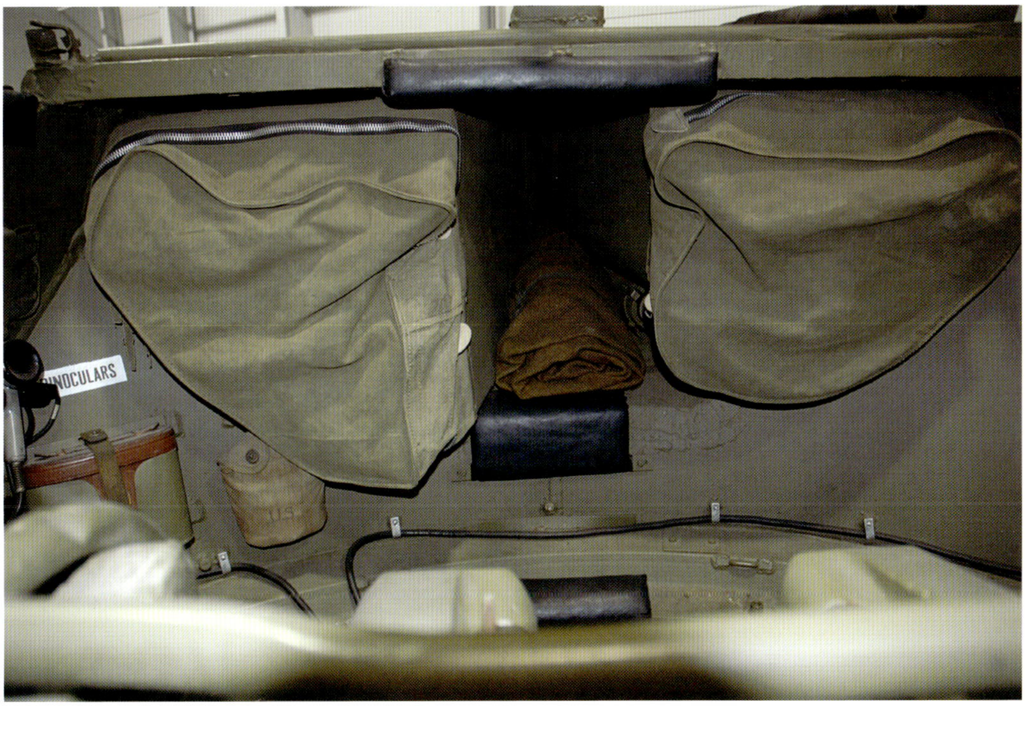
INOCULARS

Above: The stowage on the left side forward turret wall includes from left to right: the power cord reel for the spotlight, a flashlight, two canteens, an M2 decontamination unit, and a portable 4lb fire extinguisher.

Opposite above: The center of the turret is dominated by the M3 90mm gun's breech end and recoil guard. The partial turret floor for the gunner and commander can be seen below the gun at the right front of the turret.

Opposite below: The post at top left is the elevating gear for the gun. The link at the center of the turret roof is the internal travel lock which holds the breech end firmly in place when the barrel is in the rear gun crutch.

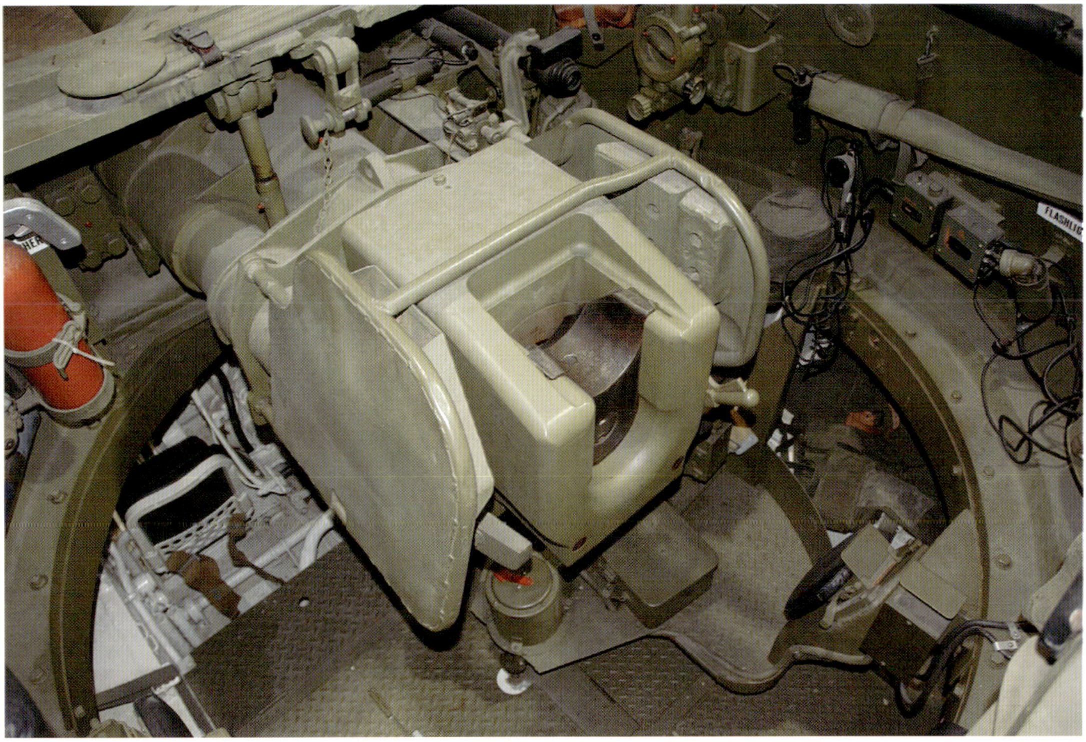

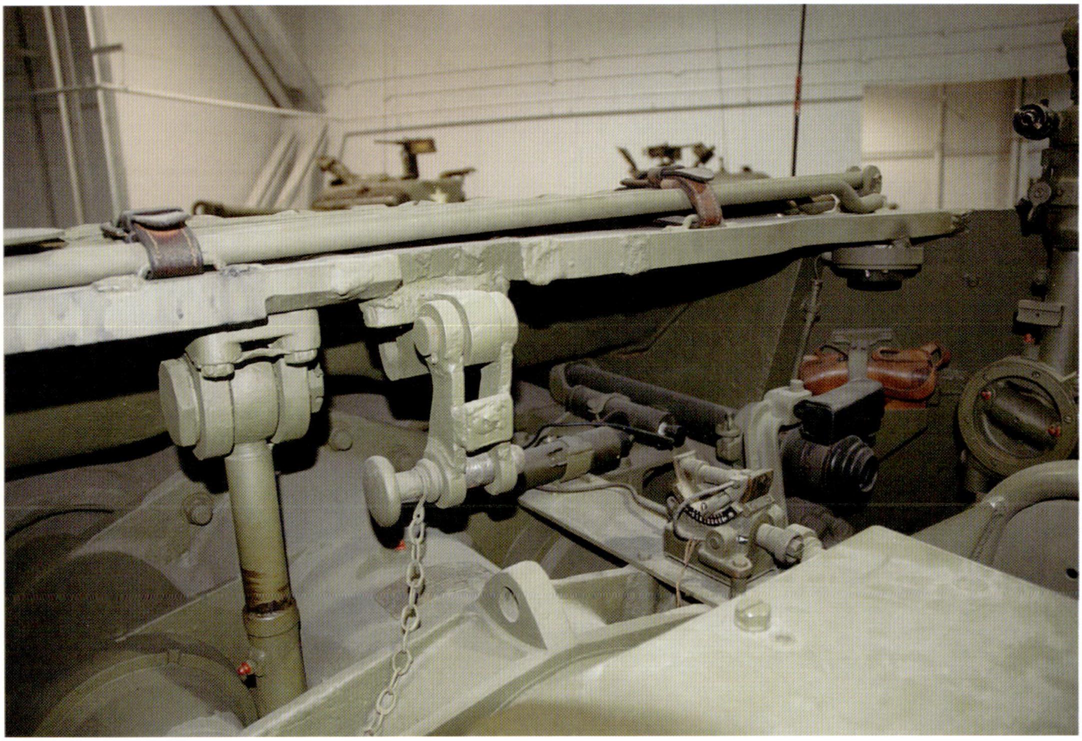

Above: The pintle mount for the .50-caliber machine gun is fastened to a square plate tapped for four screws, which is welded to the top of the bustle. The pintle mount is hinged at its base to allow it to lie flat when the gun is not mounted. The round plug on the chain by the pintle base covers the opening at the top of the pintle when the gun is removed.

Opposite above: The Browning M2 .50-caliber machine gun on an M36 tank destroyer is viewed close-up from the left front, focusing on the receiver. At the front of the top of the receiver is the front sight with a bow-shaped glare shield over it. At the rear top of the receiver is the rear sight, a folding, leaf-type design. At the rear of the receiver are the two grips.

Opposite below: On the left side of the M2 .50-caliber machine gun is a 105-round ammunition box; it is seated on a tray assembly that is mounted on a bracket fastened to the gun cradle. On the outer side of the tray is a sprung clamp assembly that acts to hold the ammo box in place. When the cover of the box is removed to feed ammunition into the machine gun, the clamp serves to hold down the linked ammunition in the box.

D11

105 CAL. .50
LINKED
API M8
REPACKED LOT
COD-L88136

Above: A rack for the stowage of two spare barrels for the machine gun is located on the left side of the bustle, and the folding travel lock brace for the machine gun barrel is at the right rear. Note the bustle's cast texture.

Opposite above: The ranging poles, or aiming stakes, are stowed on each side of the turret bustle through the turret lift rings. The lower stake has a sharp end for driving into the ground, the upper stake's end inserts into the other.

Opposite below: Below the spare barrel mount on the turret bustle is a bracket which clamps around the cooling jacket at the front end of the .50 caliber machine gun's receiver when the gun is stored on the turret rear.

Above: The engine oil cooler is mounted at the center of the firewall at the rear of the fighting compartment. The cover below the cooler is for the bulge of the clutch assembly. The drive shaft runs below the floor to the transmission.

Opposite above: The main ammunition stowage is in four cavities within the hull sponsons. Thirty-six rounds are stacked in their fiber packing tubes and lashed in place with web straps; this brings the vehicle total to 47.

Opposite below: The floor of the fighting compartment is made up of hinged panels with an anti-slip tread plate surface. The loader's seat hangs from the turret ring. The turret electrical connections come up through the center of the floor.

Above: The instrument panel includes the following gauges, from top left: volts, amps, tachometer with engine hours, bottom left to right, fuel level, coolant temp, speedometer with odometer, oil pressure, and oil temp.

Opposite above: Steering of the M36 was accomplished by steering brakes located in the differentials between the transmission and the final drives. In a view of the driver's compartment of an M36, the steering-brake levers are to the front of the driver's seat. To the front of the levers are two steering rods, the left steering brake and differential housing. To the upper left is the instrument panel and to the right is the transmission. The gearshift lever is in the right foreground.

Opposite below: In a driver's-eye view of the upper part of the driver's compartment, the driver's hatch is to the left; the driver's and assistant driver's intercom/radio control boxes, cords, and microphones are to the center; and the assistant driver's hatch is to the right, with the periscope on the hatch door visible. Two canteens are stored below the intercom boxes.

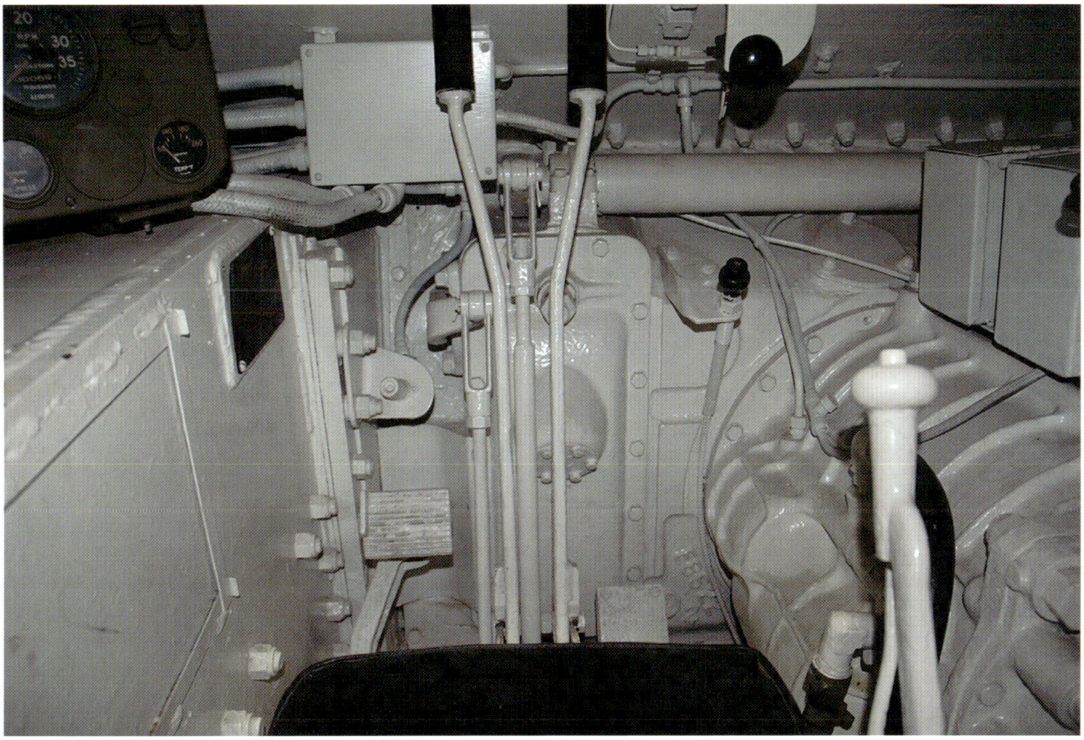

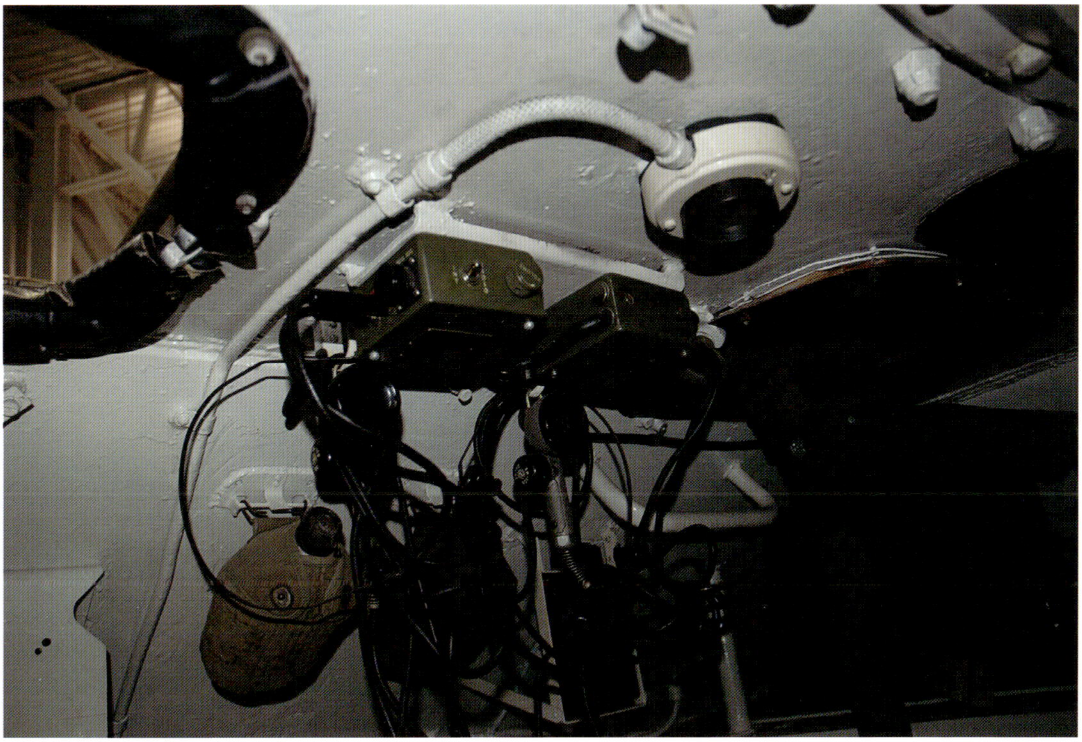

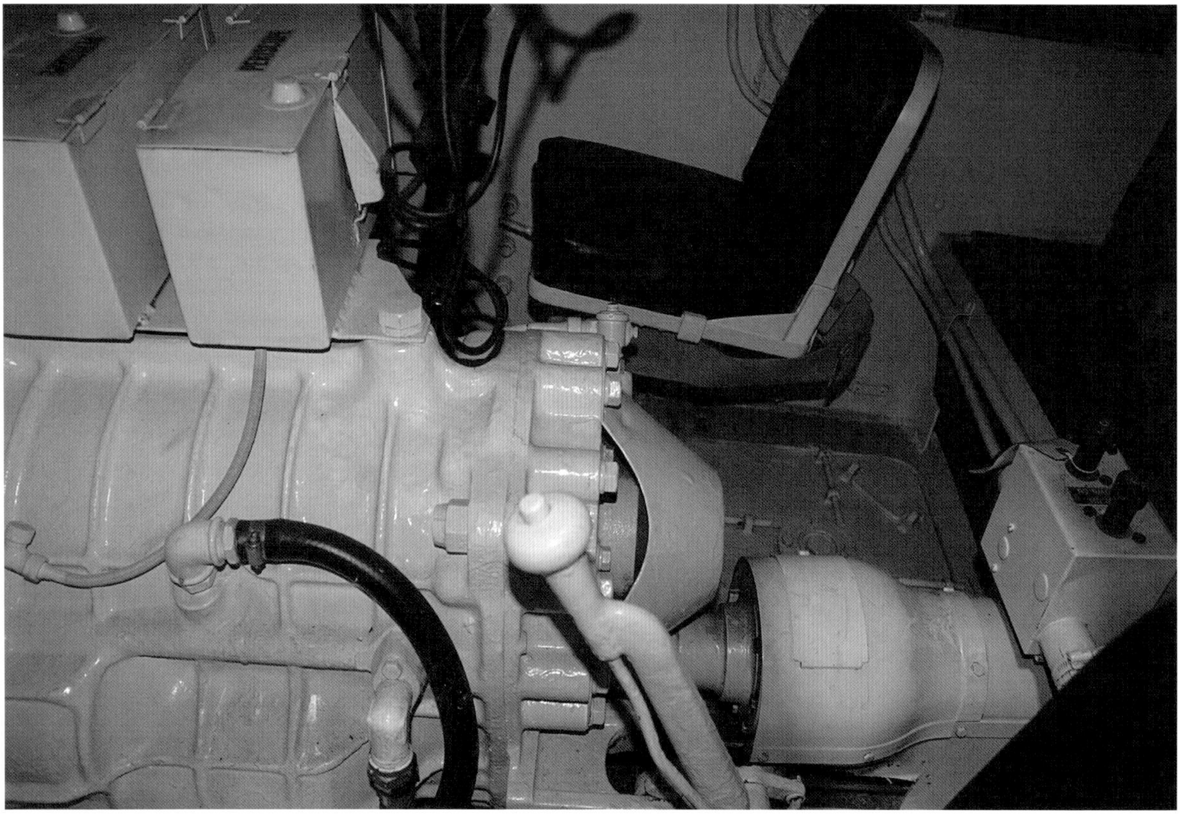

Above: The five-speed transmission is at the front of the vehicle with its connection to the drive shaft at its rear. The shift lever is in the foreground with a lock-out button on the end for first gear and reverse.

Opposite above: The factory-installed radio for the M36 and M10 was the SCR-610, which is mounted in the right front sponson and operated by the assistant driver. The radio was also tied into the RC-99 interphone system.

Opposite below: Mounted behind and above the transmission is the main electrical control box. The two handles lock down to turn the power on for the vehicle. The assistant driver's position is seen beyond the transmission.

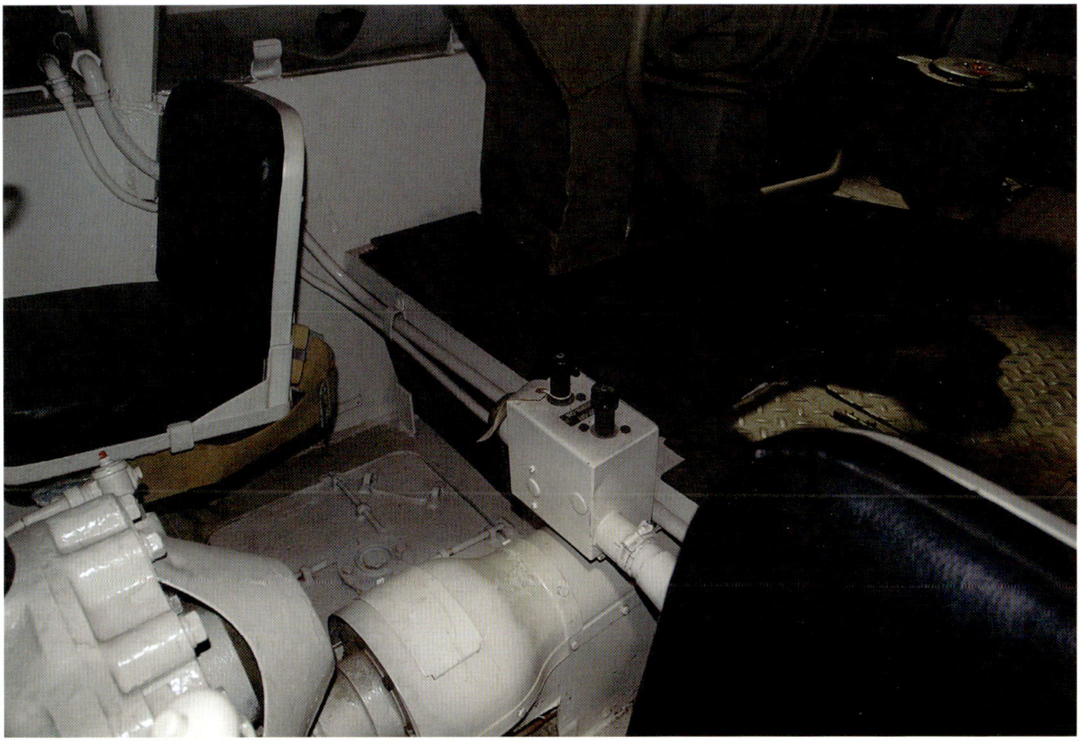

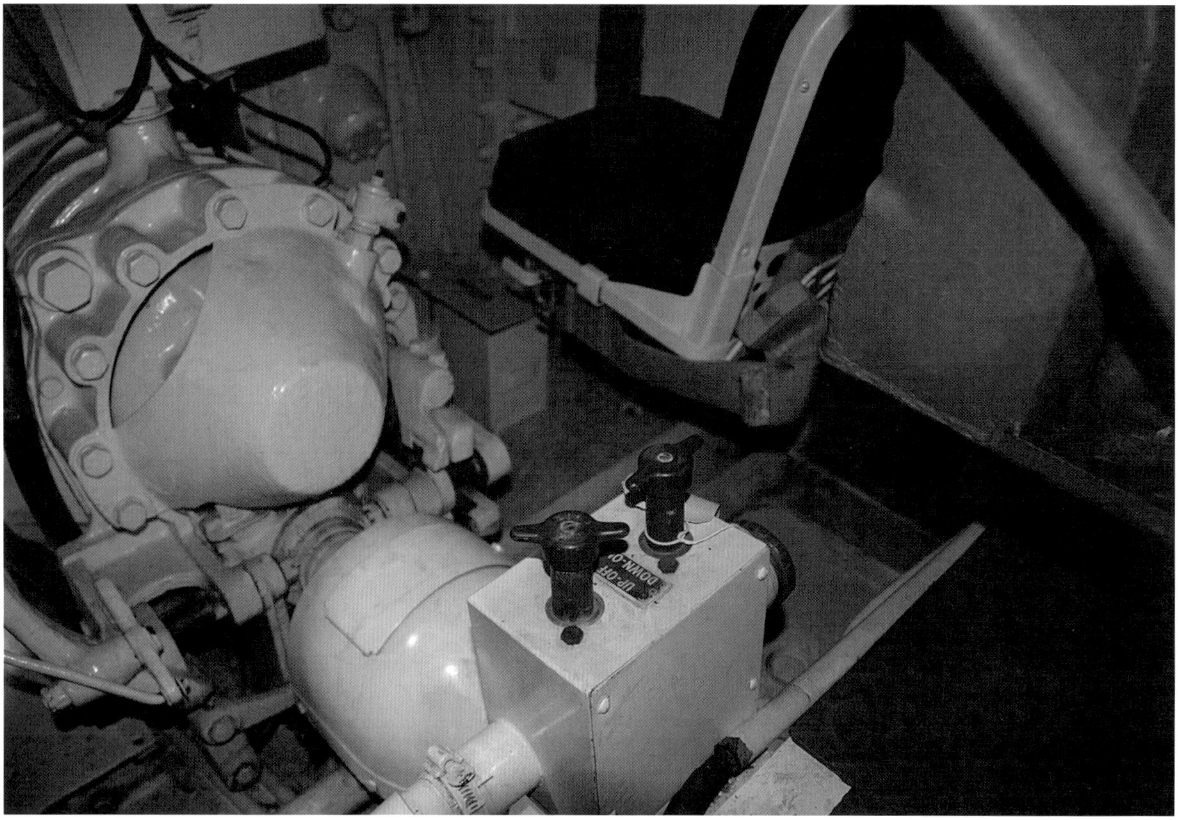

Above: The main electrical control box is seen here from the rear. Below the conical cover at the upper rear of the transmission is a power take-off which is used to run a generator.

Opposite above: Directly behind the assistant driver is located the partial turret floor below the gunner's feet. The gunner stays in a fixed position relative to the gun as the turret rotates. The pipes are hydraulic fittings for the power traverse.

Opposite below: The pump motor for the power traverse is mounted just below the control box for the hydraulics. The elevation gear is seen in the foreground with the pistol grip control for the mechanism behind.

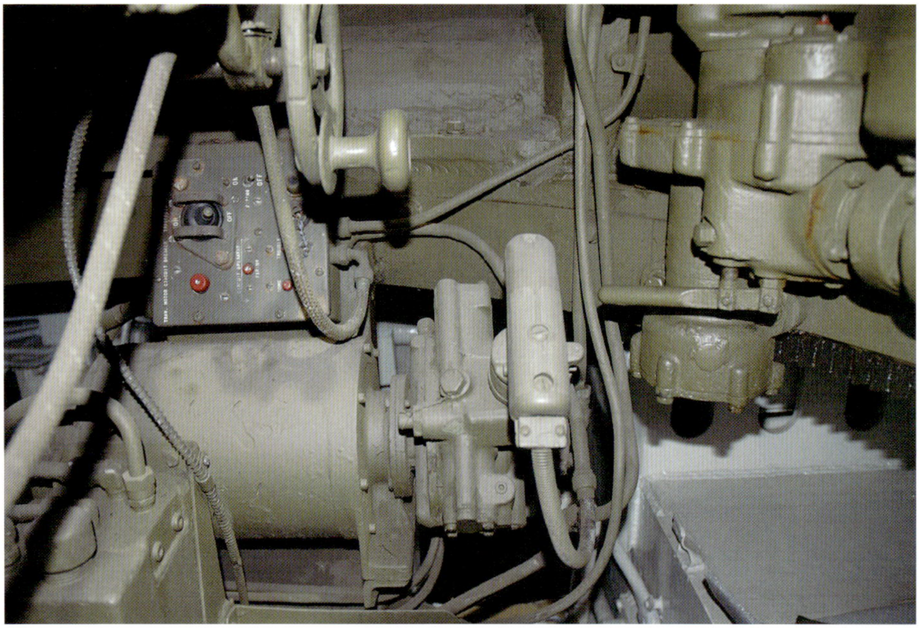

The control box is equipped with the switches for the hydraulic pump as well as the electrical connections for firing the main gun. The elevation hand wheel is to the right of the box, the pistol grip traverse control at center.

The M36's power traverse could completely rotate the turret in fifteen seconds. It also eliminated the problem experienced in the earlier M10 of increased effort needed to rotate the turret while on a slope.

CHAPTER 2

M36B1

In the months after D-Day, there was an increasing demand for 90mm-armed tank destroyers, but a limited supply of M10s available for conversion. However, at that time there was a surplus of M4A3 medium tank chassis, and these were compatible with the M36 turret. Thus, in the final quarter of 1944, Fisher converted 187 M4A3s to 90mm-armed tank destroyers, designated the M36B1 and classified as substitute standard. (Patton Museum)

Above: M36B1 USA number 40191054 is viewed from above during tests at Aberdeen Proving Ground, Maryland, on 26 December 26. The M4A3 medium tank was automotively identical to the M36, and the conversion mainly required modifications to the storage of 90mm ammunition in the hull and the relocation of the radio to the forward part of the right sponson in the assistant driver's compartment. The X-shaped frame on the turret presumably was a support for a canvas turret cover that was experimented with in late 1944. (NARA)

Opposite above: M36B1 40191054 is parked at Aberdeen Proving Ground with the turret traversed to the rear and the 90mm gun resting in the travel lock, on 21 December 1944. An M3 muzzle brake, a dual-baffle model, was fitted to the gun, and the gunner's sight aperture on the mantlet has been covered with tape or sealant. The canvas cover for the turret is installed, fastened with straps to footman loops on the turret side. This turret cover, naturally, was not necessary on 90mm-armed tank destroyers with armored turret covers. (NARA)

Opposite below: The M36B1 undergoing analysis at Aberdeen Proving Ground in December 1944 is viewed from the front. From this angle an enemy gunner could have mistaken this vehicle for a 76mm-armed Sherman tank. A clear view is available of the M3 muzzle brake from the front. (NARA)

The crew of an M36B1 of the 654th Tank Destroyer Battalion pose for their photograph in Rheinberg, Germany, on 6 March 1945. The 90mm gun was fitted with a muzzle collar in lieu of a muzzle brake. Duckbill end connectors are on the outboard side of the tracks. A .50-caliber machine gun on a pintle mount is on the left front of the turret, and four small Nazi flags, likely indicating kills, are affixed to the mantlet above the gunner's sight aperture. (Patton Museum)

This M36B1 tank destroyer has become mired and has thrown its left track along a road near Hargarten, Germany, on 15 March 1945. Two members of the crew kill time by writing letters home while waiting for a wrecker to arrive. These GIs were members of the 899th Tank Destroyer Battalion, attached to the 9th Infantry Division. (NARA)

This rare surviving M36B1 is on display at the 4th Infantry Division Museum, Fort Hood, Texas. It is armed with a 90mm gun M3A1, a postwar model with a muzzle brake and a bore evacuator on the barrel. This vehicle has a mix of solid-disk and open-spoke bogie wheels: a mix that would not have been abnormal during active-service use.

Many M36s were modernized after the end of the Second World War, receiving the M3A1 90mm gun, also used on the M46 Patton. The new gun was equipped with a single baffle muzzle brake and a fume extractor on the barrel.

The M36B1s were constructed at the same time as the large hatch M4A3 hulls that were coming off the Fisher assembly lines in late 1944, and share many details. These incorporated many late features such as the lift rings positioned on the outer edge of the glacis.

The fume extractor, or bore evacuator, creates a low pressure situation in the gun barrel after a round is fired. This eliminates the risk of a flash back into the interior of the vehicle when the breech is opened.

The turret on the M36B1 was identical to the standard M36. The General Motors Fisher Tank Arsenal built a total of 187 M36B1s in the last three months of 1944. They were issued to the same units as M36s.

The raised wire guard for the driver's periscope is a common post-war modification to M36 variants. The glacis armor of the M36B1 was 2½ inches thick while the upper hull sides are 1½, both thicker than the M36.

The removal of the gun assembly affords a rare view of the complete recoil assembly of the M3 90mm gun. This powerful weapon had a range of 21,000 yards and armor penetration of over eight inches depending on ammunition. (David Levy)

The large turret front casting that incorporates the gun trunions is completely exposed once the gun is fully removed. The threaded holes are evident where the cast roof section attaches to the turret front. (David Levy)

The pictured example is preserved at Fort Hood in Texas where so many tank destroyer units trained during the Second World War. The vehicle is equipped with the standard VVSS suspension of the M4A3 with the late upswept arms for the return roller. The strip along the lower edge of the hull side armor is for mounting a sand shield. Remnants of the sand shield remain attached to the front fenders.

The left side glacis has the standard headlight mount and guard, along with a conduit opening for a missing siren. Just above the lift ring is a U-shaped bracket for mounting a rear view mirror, a late M4A3 feature.

Although tank destroyer units were quickly disbanded in the US Army after the Second World War, the weapons themselves were still quite formidable. Many were supplied to friendly armies through the Military Assistance Program. (David Levy)

The turret design of the M36 was much better balanced than the earlier M10. The bustle was designed as a thick casting to eliminate the need of any additional external counterweights.

The turret bustle has a T-shaped cross section when viewed from the rear. The bracket at the center of the bustle is for storing the broken down .50 caliber machine gun, with the clamp to the left holding the cooling jacket in place.

Above left: The cast lift rings are welded to the sides of the turret bustle and the welds have been ground down. The brackets are for storage of aiming stakes. Note the weld seams where the bustle joins the turret walls.

Above right: The only distinguishing feature of the M36B1 hull from that of the standard M4A3 hull is the rear-mounted gun travel lock. Late-M4A3 features include the rear storage rack, spare track racks, and engine door props.

This M36B1 tank destroyer was in Iraq during the US invasion of that country. It formerly served with the Iranian army and was captured during the Iran-Iraq War in the 1980s. Although some of the sheet metal was crumpled, the exterior of the vehicle was in a fairly good state of repair. (David Levy)

Above: The engine compartment of the captured Iranian/Iraqi M36B1 shows signs of decades of neglect, with much rust and dust. The hoses from the air cleaners on the front bulkhead to the air-intake manifold on the Ford GAA V-8 engine are missing. Above the engine compartment, details of the weld beads securing the bustle to the turret are visible. (Jay Ehmann via David Levvy)

Opposite above: The engine deck doors of this M36B1 are open revealing the sheet metal baffles attached to the underside of the engine grills. These baffles redirected cooling air over the motor towards the radiators at the rear of the compartment. (Geoff Walden via David Levy)

Opposite below: The upper portion of the splash rail on the forward edge of the engine deck is notched for turret clearance on the M36B1. The base of the turret is provided 360-degree protection by the splash rail casting of the upper hull. (Geoff Walden via David Levy)

This M36B1 is undergoing restoration. Another feature of the M36B1 hull is the bracket on the front glacis beside the right headlight for the antenna mount. This was made necessary when the SCR-610 radio was relocated to the co-driver sponson. The M36B1 was the only tank destroyer equipped with a bow machine gun, retaining the one from the M4A3. (David Levy)

Although the US Army's doctrine that brought about the tank destroyer may have been flawed, the weapons themselves proved effective and versatile. They provided an armor-piercing punch on the battlefields of North Africa, Italy, and north-west Europe superior to the M4. Allied troops and commanders found uses for the weapons for which they were never intended. After the war the vehicles were provided to numerous armies including the Danish, French, Dutch, and Korean. Their long combat history continued on into Viet Nam with the French, and with the struggles in the Balkans in the 1990s. This M36 was found in Iraq during Operation Iraqi Freedom. (Jay Ehmann via David Levy)